Brain and Cognition

Some New Technologies

Daniel Druckman and John I. Lacey, *Editors*

Committee on New Technologies in Cognitive Psychophysiology
Commission on Behavioral and Social Sciences and Education
National Research Council

NATIONAL ACADEMY PRESS
Washington, DC   1989

NOTICE: The project that is the subject of this report was approved by the Governing Board of the National Research Council, whose members are drawn from the councils of the National Academy of Sciences, the National Academy of Engineering, and the Institute of Medicine. The members of the committee responsible for the report were chosen for their special competences and with regard for appropriate balance.

This report has been reviewed by a group other than the authors according to procedures approved by a Report Review Committee consisting of members of the National Academy of Sciences, the National Academy of Engineering, and the Institute of Medicine.

The National Academy of Sciences is a private, nonprofit, self-perpetuating society of distinguished scholars engaged in scientific and engineering research, dedicated to the furtherance of science and technology and to their use for the general welfare. Upon the authority of the charter granted to it by the Congress in 1863, the Academy has a mandate that requires it to advise the federal government on scientific and technical matters. Dr. Frank Press is president of the National Academy of Sciences.

The National Academy of Engineering was established in 1964, under the charter of the National Academy of Sciences, as a parallel organization of outstanding engineers. It is autonomous in its administration and in the selection of its members, sharing with the National Academy of Sciences the responsibility for advising the federal government. The National Academy of Engineering also sponsors engineering programs aimed at meeting national needs, encourages education and research, and recognizes the superior achievements of engineers. Dr. Robert M. White is president of the National Academy of Engineering.

The Institute of Medicine was established in 1970 by the National Academy of Sciences to secure the services of eminent members of appropriate professions in the examination of policy matters pertaining to the health of the public. The Institute acts under the responsibility given to the National Academy of Sciences by its congressional charter to be an adviser to the federal government and, upon its own initiative, to identify issues of medical care, research, and education. Dr. Samuel O. Thier is president of the Institute of Medicine.

The National Research Council was organized by the National Academy of Sciences in 1916 to associate the broad community of science and technology with the Academy's purposes of furthering knowledge and advising the federal government. Functioning in accordance with general policies determined by the Academy, the Council has become the principal operating agency of both the National Academy of Sciences and the National Academy of Engineering in providing services to the government, the public, and the scientific and engineering communities. The Council is administered jointly by both Academies and the Institute of Medicine. Dr. Frank Press and Dr. Robert M. White are chairman and vice chairman, respectively, of the National Research Council.

This report was sponsored by the United States Army Research Institute.

Available from:
Committee on New Technologies in Cognitive Psychophysiology
National Research Council
2101 Constitution Avenue N.W.
Washington, D.C. 20418

COMMITTEE ON NEW TECHNOLOGIES IN COGNITIVE PSYCHOPHYSIOLOGY

JOHN I. LACEY (NAS) (Chair), Department of Psychology, Wright State University (retired) (psychophysiology)
EMANUEL DONCHIN, Department of Psychology, University of Illinois, Champaign (cognitive psychophysiology)
MICHAEL S. GAZZANIGA, Department of Psychiatry, Dartmouth Medical School (cognitive neuroscience, memory)
LLOYD KAUFMAN, Department of Psychology, New York University (neuromagnetism, psychophysiology)
STEPHEN M. KOSSLYN, Department of Psychology, Harvard University (cognitive neuroscience)
MARCUS E. RAICHLE, Division of Radiation Science, Mallinckrodt Institute, Washington University (neurology)

DANIEL DRUCKMAN, Study Director (experimental social psychology)
ALISON J. FOLEY, Administrative Secretary
DONNA REIFSNIDER, Administrative Secretary

Preface

As a part of its mission to apply modern technology to military problems, the Army Research Institute (ARI) asked the National Academy of Sciences/National Research Council, in its primary role as science advisers to the federal government, to evaluate recent technical developments in the monitoring of brain activity for their relevance to basic and applied issues relating to the acquisition and maintenance of cognitive skills. Accordingly, the Commission on Behavioral and Social Sciences and Education within the National Research Council considered the proposal. The area to be reviewed is a part of its continuing surveillance of the exploding field of psychobiology, particularly the areas of learning and memory; the proposal provided an incentive to explore in detail a part of this vast interdisciplinary venture. It was felt that a preliminary review could result in an informed opinion, one based on actual experience with the technologies, concerning the desirability, feasibility, and utility of a larger continuing study of the relations between neuroscience and cognitive science.

The commission appointed a small Committee on New Technologies in Cognitive Psychophysiology, specifying that its work was to be completed within the period of one year. The committee was asked not only to conduct the requested review, but also, if it seemed appropriate, to develop plans for a larger, broader, and continuing study. The committee was requested also to suggest ways for ARI to monitor developments in the field of cognitive psychophysiology.

The committee members were selected both for their acknowledged expertise in one of the specific technologies covered in this report and for their breadth of contribution to interdisciplinary theory and research. These contributors and their areas of primary responsibility were: Emanuel Donchin, event-related potentials; Michael S. Gazzaniga, studies of brain damage; Lloyd Kaufman, the magnetoencephalogram; Stephen M. Kosslyn, cognitive psychology and cognitive science (with emphasis on one form of interface with computer science); and Marcus E. Raichle, brain imaging (positron emission tomography and magnetic resonance imaging). Overall editorial responsibility for the report was taken by Daniel Druckman, an experimental social psychologist who was study director for the project, and myself, a psychophysiologist.

The committee met together twice. The first session was devoted to a briefing from the ARI and then to detailed consideration of the structure and content of the report. Each member outlined the essence of the state of his assigned field and the interrelationships with the other areas of study. Through extensive discussions, a preliminary common format was agreed upon, and writing tasks were assigned. This was followed by an extensive period of writing, submission and circulation of drafts, and preliminary revisions. The telephone and computer were the main vehicles of communication among the committee members, study director Daniel Druckman, and myself.

A second meeting was held toward the end of the year, for purposes of melding the separate materials into a more coherent whole, of arriving at a consensus concerning controversial points, and for assessing the future of this preliminary venture and making appropriate recommendations. It was followed by a final period of rewriting and editorial work, again aided by extensive use of telephone and modem.

The report draws on a variety of techniques and concepts from diverse fields of research. We ask for the reader's patience in making his or her way through this technical material concerning an emerging interdisciplinary field. Dr. Druckman and I bear the responsibility for any editorial deficiencies that remain, and we are grateful for the careful reviews of the report by the Commission Behavioral and Social Sciences and Education and the Report Review Committee.

On a personal note, I express profound thanks to Dr. Druckman for his skilled and professional support of this venture. Special thanks and acknowledgments are made to the administrative secretaries

Alison Foley and Donna Reifsnider and to Christine L. McShane, who carefully edited the entire report.

>John I. Lacey
>Chair, Committee on New Technologies in
>Cognitive Psychophysiology

Contents

ABBREVIATIONS		xi
SUMMARY OF CONCLUSIONS AND RECOMMENDATIONS		1
1	INTRODUCTION	5
2	THE FIELD OF COGNITIVE PSYCHOPHYSIOLOGY	7
3	FOUR NEW TECHNOLOGIES: RESEARCH FINDINGS	18
4	FOUR NEW TECHNOLOGIES: CRITICAL PROBLEMS	43
5	APPLICATIONS AND ETHICAL CONSIDERATIONS	60
6	EXPANDING THE DOMAIN	65
REFERENCES		69

Abbreviations

ANS	Autonomic nervous system
ATP	Adenisone triphosphate
^{13}C	A nonradioactive form of carbon whose atomic weight is 13
CNS	Central nervous system
CT	X-ray computed tomography
EEG	Electroencephalogram
ERF	Event-related fields
ERP	Event-related brain potentials
EF	Evoked fields
^{18}F	A radioactive form of flourine whose atomic weight is 18
Pi	Inorganic phosphate
MEG	Magnetoencephalography
MRI	Magnetic resonance imaging
MRS	Magnetic resonance spectroscopy
N100	A negative component of the ERP occurring with a modal latency of 100 mec
N300	A negative component of the ERP occurring with a modal latency of 300 msec
^{23}Na	A nonradioactive form of sodium whose atomic weight is 23
^{15}O	A radioactive form of oxygen whose atomic weight in 15

P300	A positive component of the ERP occurring with a modal latency of 300 msec
PET	Positron emission tomography
^{31}P	A nonradioactive form of phosphorous whose atomic weight is 31
pH	A measure of hydrogen ion concentration in the tissue
PCr	Phosphocreatin
SQUID	Superconducting quantum interference device

Summary of Conclusions and Recommendations

In response to a request from the U.S. Army Research Institute (ARI), the National Research Council (NRC) formed a committee to undertake a preliminary study of the development of the major new technologies in cognitive psychophysiology. The task of the committee, to be accomplished within one year, was to examine four technologies: (1) event-related brain potentials (ERPs), (2) the magnetoencephalogram (MEG), (3) the brain-imaging techniques of positron emission tomography (PET) and magnetic resonance image (MRI), and (4) the approach based on studying patients with brain lesions or damage. For each technology, the committee identified critical problems that must be resolved if further progress is to be made; estimated the likelihood that such progress will be made; and discussed opportunities for basic and applied research. The committee also discussed the implementation of an enlarged discipline called cognitive neuroscience that combines psychophysiology, cognitive psychology, and computer modeling.

The technologies examined by the committee hold considerable promise for furthering our understanding of the brain and cognition. Electrical, metabolic, and structural definition of specific cognitive states is increasing at a rapid rate. Clearly, the technologies discussed in this report will play a major role in the further development of theories of the neural mechanisms of human cognition. Any major agency involved in personnel training would be well advised to participate in research programs that either contribute to or keep them abreast of advances in this field.

Available evidence suggests that it may be possible to develop measures of brain activity during cognition, already studied under laboratory conditions, to be used as indices in personnel selection and training in the military context. However, to extend the use of these measures (both those already studied in detail and those in the pipeline) to practical applications, well-designed normative and validation studies in the field will be required. The cost of such implementations will have to be weighed against the anticipated benefits in specific situations. Rather than being used for selection and training, in the near future it is more likely that the brain technologies will serve as important tools in the development of cognitive theory and in discovering the specific skills to be assessed.

The committee's recommendations highlight several areas for attention:

- The committee recommends that a research program be developed to examine applications of event-related potentials to problems in field environments. This technology is the one most ready for practical use. Particularly promising possibilities exist in the monitoring of the direction of attention, in the measurement of mental workload, and in monitoring performance in missions of long duration.
- The committee recommends simultaneous and complementary use of the technologies. This would permit investigators to benefit from the different advantages of, for example, PET and MRI or ERP and MEG. Such complementarity may lead to stronger conclusions about relationships between physiological and cognitive processes than are currently available.
- The committee recommends that data be obtained on the range of variability in functional and structural maps across and within individuals. A functional and structural map refers to the distribution of brain activity in the three spatial dimensions as a function of time. Such a map would best be based on the complementary data provided by PET, MRI, and electrical and magnetic recordings and should be used for testing computational models of human cognition, as defined in this report. In addition, further research is needed to increase understanding of the dynamic patterns of activity in cortical neuronal processing as they relate to human behavior.
- The committee recommends consideration of postdoctoral training programs to encourage interdisciplinary research in cognitive neuroscience.

- In view of the high cost and complex operations of some of the imaging technologies, the committee recommends that consideration be given to the development, in these areas, of national facilities that will support the research of both local and remote investigators.
- The committee concludes that the time is ripe for a hybrid psychophysiological-cognitive science approach to the study of brain functions and behavior and recommends an enlarged study of the interrelationship between cognitive science and neuroscience.

1
Introduction

In response to a request from the U.S. Army Research Institute (ARI), a National Research Council (NRC) committee was formed to undertake, over a one-year period, a study of new technologies in cognitive psychophysiology, particularly with respect to potential applications to military problems. The committee was asked to carry out the following tasks: review and assess current research relevant to issues concerning the relationship between the new technologies and cognitive skills; on the basis of this review, assess the likelihood that progress will be made in the foreseeable future; identify opportunities for basic and applied research with proper recognition of ethical issues; and assess the feasibility and desirability of a major study on the relation between cognitive science and neuroscience.

Because of the study's time limitations, this report covers only the four technologies that were examined by the committee: (1) event-related brain potentials (ERPs), (2) the magnetoencephalogram (MEG), (3) brain-imaging techniques (PET and MRI), and (4) the approach based on studying patients with brain lesions or disconnections, usually caused by accidents or traumas. The committee considered the critical conceptual and empirical problems facing the field as well as potential opportunities provided by the technologies for better understanding of cognitive processes. The discussion in this report of these basic and applied issues is the basis for the committee's recommendations.

Following this introduction, the report is organized into five chapters. Chapter 2 is an attempt to define the field of cognitive psychophysiology, distinguishing first between cognitive psychology on one hand and psychophysiology on the other, and then discussing the advantages of combining the two into an enlarged discipline. Chapter 3 consists of a detailed discussion of each of the technologies, including a review of current research, appraisals of the likelihood of progress, and a discussion of opportunities for future research. Chapter 4 discusses problems that must be resolved if progress is to be made. Chapter 5 deals with applications and ethical issues. Chapter 6 considers the feasibility of an enlarged study of the relation between cognitive science and neuroscience.

This structure is intended to facilitate the task of reading the report. Discussions of the four technologies are found in two chapters: Chapter 3 presents a description of each technology, a discussion of methodological issues, and a review of relevant empirical research. Chapter 4 discusses problems and issues concerning the use of each technology for research and application. The reader with more background in the areas under study will find this part to be of special interest.

2
The Field of Cognitive Psychophysiology

In this chapter we define cognitive psychophysiology in terms of its two parts, cognitive science and psychophysiology.

WHAT IS COGNITIVE SCIENCE?

The *Oxford Dictionary of the English Language* defines cognition as "the action or faculty of knowing taken in its widest sense, including sensation, perception, conception, as distinguished from feeling and volition; also, more specifically, the action of cognizing an object in perception proper." Thus, cognitive science is the body of scientific knowledge pertaining to cognition, defined to include all forms of knowing.

Cognitive science focuses on questions about how information must be stored internally and processed in order for an organism to recognize objects, learn, use language, reason, or navigate. Theories are tested in part by attempting to build computer programs that mimic human performance (the so-called computational approach) and in part by using the experimental methods of cognitive psychology.

The computational approach characterizes the nature of information processing at two levels of analysis. At one level, theorists decompose the processing system into sets of "processing modules," each of which performs some part of the processing used to accomplish a task. Modules are "black boxes," specifying how specific types of input are transformed to produce appropriate output. Sternberg

(1969), for example, postulated one module that compares an input stimulus in short-term memory to a set of items on a list.

At another level, theorists attempt to discover the way in which processing is actually accomplished within the modules. In some cases processing is characterized by step-by-step sequential manipulation of stored symbols, as is done in conventional computers, whereas in other cases, processing corresponds to the formation of patterns of activation in a network of interconnected nodes, as is done in parallel distributed processing systems (Rumelhart and McClelland, 1986). For example, the list-comparison module posited by Sternberg could operate either by storing the items in memory as symbols in a list and then comparing an input symbol against each stored symbol, or by establishing a pattern of weights distributed through a neural network. In this latter case, comparison of input to stored items is accomplished simply by discovering whether the network settles into a specific state when a given input is presented. In either case, the computational approach leads one to posit a set of modules and to characterize how they serve to transform information.

Cognitive psychology has contributed to cognitive science sophisticated methodologies, a rich data base on characteristics of human performance, and techniques for modeling such data. The methodologies of cognitive psychology are based on observing relative response times, error rates, or types of judgments. For example, cognitive psychologists have developed techniques for inferring properties of processing by analyzing trade-offs between speed and accuracy (i.e., the inverse relationship between times and errors, which reflects how careful a subject is when responding); they have used signal detection theory in the analysis of errors to determine what is stored. They have also developed numerous methods for obtaining judgments of perceived similarity among stimuli. These judgments in turn can be submitted to multidimensional scaling and cluster analyses, allowing one to draw inferences about the processing underlying the judgments. Hypotheses derived from theories that embody different modular structures or types of processing are tested against data. For example, if there is a discrete module that compares input to lists stored in short-term memory, then it should be possible to find brain-damaged patients with focal lesions who have lost this specific ability. In short, then, the result of the alliance between computational theorizing and cognitive psychology is the development of detailed theories of information processing that are not only consistent with the available data about human performance, but that also make empirically testable predictions (see Anderson, 1983; Kosslyn, 1980; Rumelhart and McClelland, 1986).

WHAT IS PSYCHOPHYSIOLOGY?

Cognitive psychophysiology refers to the study and use of measures of physiological functions for the purpose of elucidating processes and mechanisms that underlie cognition. The physiological processes studied include both central nervous system (CNS) and autonomic nervous system (ANS) activities. Traditionally, psychophysiologists interested in the ANS measure such variables as changes in heart rate or sweat gland activity (Coles, Donchin, and Porges, 1986). Studies of the CNS have been dominant in cognitive psychophysiology and are based on more widely developed technologies than are studies of ANS activity related to cognition. For that reason, the report concentrates on those activities designed to clarify CNS mechanisms involved in human cognition.

The human brain is largely inaccessible to the sort of fine-grained analysis other organisms can be subjected to in the pursuit of knowledge about how neuronal activity relates to psychological processes and states. We already know enough about brain and behavioral processes to see that a full understanding of another organism is insufficient to allow a complete appreciation of how the human brain carries out its appointed tasks. While it is imperative for the student of human behavior to keep an eye on the developments in understanding brain and behavioral processes in nonhuman species, it is also becoming clear that an understanding of human psychological processes will require studying human brains at work. This is an ambitious goal and one not easy to achieve.

THE INTERFACE BETWEEN COGNITIVE SCIENCE AND PSYCHOPHYSIOLOGY

Three fields are currently engaged in the empirical study of mental activity: *computational theorists* attempt to understand seeing, remembering, reasoning, and so on by building virtual machines that mimic such processes. *Cognitive psychologists* conduct experiments to measure differences in behavior under different circumstances and attempt to fit models to account for response times, error rates, or various types of decisions. *Psychophysiologists* try to gain insight into the mind by observing the activity of its neural substrate.

In addition, it should be noted that scholars in anthropology, linguistics, and philosophy also address issues about the mind, and some aspects of cognitive science draw heavily on these fields. However, this work currently is difficult to connect to psychophysiology; hence we do not consider these facets of cognitive science further here or in the sections to follow.

Each of the three fields listed above has virtues as well as limitations. Cognitive science has to a large extent grown out of an alliance between the computational approach and cognitive psychology. The weaknesses of each field taken in isolation are to a large degree corrected for by the strengths of the others. It seems likely that psychophysiology has much to gain from interactions with this new amalgam, and vice versa.

In this section we first treat the virtues and limitations of each of the major fields, taken singly, to the study of cognition. We then propose an alliance among them, which would take advantage of each one's unique strengths—empirical, technological, and theoretical—while compensating for the limitations inherent in each single field. The section concludes with a discussion of the advantages of combining them, leading to the suggestion, made in Chapter 6, for an enlarged study of the interface between the disciplines.

Limitations and Virtues of a Psychophysiological Approach

Psychophysiological data may be especially useful for identifying the structure of information processing in the brain. But to be maximally useful, they must be used in conjunction with sophisticated theories and methodologies that are capable of discriminating among such theories.

Attempts to program computers to behave with the intelligence of even a field mouse have been of limited success. One thing we have learned from such efforts is just how complicated cognitive processing is. Even the simplest task, such as deciding whether a dot is inside or outside a closed boundary, requires sophisticated processing (Ullman, 1984). If we are to understand the neural basis of cognition, we must be prepared to formulate rather complex theories. Until very recently, however, this has not been done in psychophysiology. For example, "localizing oneself in space" is typically considered a single function in the psychophysiological literature, whereas a computationally-oriented theorist would be inclined to decompose this process into many disparate encoding, representational, and retrieval operations. Similarly, visual agnosia ("mindblindness") is described and the underlying causes of the deficit are explained by reference to damage of anatomical areas and their connections—but exactly what is done by these areas is never clearly specified.

Thus, to expand the contribution of a psychophysiological approach it is of interest to consider what the two major strands of cognitive science, computational theorizing and cognitive psychology, can offer.

Limitations and Virtues of the Computational Approach

Although the brain clearly is not a standard digital computer, brain activity can be conceptualized as the carrying out of computations.

Computational modeling of brain activity occurs at multiple levels of analysis. The most appropriate level for present purposes focuses on the decomposition of processing into modules, each of which may correspond to a distinct neural network. Any given task presumably recruits many such modules to work together, and the ways in which modules interact determines task performance. Although specifying the precise operation of the individual modules is of course critical for a theory of information processing, at the current level of technology we are unlikely to be able to use methods of assessing brain activity to directly test theories at this level of analysis. The main contribution of the computational approach to cognitive psychophysiology will therefore probably be to offer guidelines for how one formulates theories of processing modules.

An example is the work of Marr (1982): according to Marr, the most important task is to formulate the "theory of the computation," a theory of what is computed by a processing module. Marr argues that the information available and the purpose of a computation often virtually dictate what the computation must be. This sort of theory can be likened to a solution to a mathematics problem, arising through logical analysis of the nature of the problem to be solved and of the input available to solve it. That is, if the task is very well defined and the input is highly restricted, a specific computation may almost be logically necessary. Furthermore, Marr claims that once a computation is defined, the task of characterizing the representations and processes used in carrying out the step-by-step processing itself is now highly constrained: the representation of the input and the output must make explicit the information necessary for the computation to serve its purpose (e.g., picking out likely locations of edges), and the representations must be sensitive to the necessary distinctions, be stable over irrelevant distinctions, and have a number of other properties (see Marr, 1982, Chapter 5).

Marr's strong claims about the importance of the theory of the computation do seem appropriate for some of the problems of low-level vision, but only because there are such severe constraints on the input posed by the nature of the world and the geometry of surfaces and because the purpose of a computation is so well defined (e.g., to detect places where intensity changes rapidly, to derive depth from disparities in the images striking each eye, to recover structure from information about changes on a surface as an object moves).

In broader areas of cognition, the situation is different. First, the basic abilities in need of explanation, analogous to our ability to see edges or to see depth, must be discovered. For example, with the advent of new methodologies, our picture of what can be accomplished in mental imagery has changed drastically (e.g., see Shepard and Cooper, 1982). Second, the input to a "mental" computation is often not obvious, not necessarily being constrained by some easily observed property of the stimulus. One must have a theory of what is represented before one can even begin to specify the input to the computations. Third, the optimal computation will depend in part on the kinds of processing operations that are available and the type of representation used. For example, if a parallel-distributed processing network is used, computing the degree to which an input is similar to stored information should be relatively easy, whereas serial search through a list will be more difficult—and vice versa if symbols are stored as discrete elements in lists that are operated on by distinct processes.

The consequences of these difficulties are illustrated by problems with some of Marr's own work on "higher-level" vision. Marr posits that shapes must be stored using "object-centered" descriptions, as opposed to "viewer-centered" descriptions. In an object-centered description, an object is described relative to itself, not from a particular point of view. Thus, terms such as *dorsal* and *ventral* would be used in an object-centered description, rather than *top* and *bottom*, which would be used in a viewer-centered description. Marr argues that because objects are seen from so many different points of view, it would be difficult to recognize an object by matching viewer-centered descriptions to stored representations. However, this argument rests on assumptions about the kinds of processing operations that are available. If there is an "orientation normalization" preprocessor, for example, the argument is obviated: in this case, a viewer-centered description could be normalized (e.g., so the longest axis is always vertical) before matching to stored representations. And in fact, we do mentally rotate objects to a standard orientation when subtle judgments must be made (see Shepard and Cooper, 1982). The fact that we do seem to normalize the represented orientation, at least in some cases, casts doubt on the power or generality of object-centered representations. In fact, when the matter was put to empirical test, Jolicoeur and Kosslyn (1983) found that people can use both viewer-centered and object-centered coordinate systems in storing information, and they seem to encode a viewer-centered one even when they also encode an object-centered one, but not vice versa.

The point is that a logical analysis of the computation is not enough. At least for high-level cognitive functions, the specifics of a computation will depend to some extent on what types of processing operations are available in the system. One can only discover the actual state of affairs empirically, by studying the way the brain works.

Although the computational approach is not sufficient in itself to lead one to formulate a correct theory of information processing, it does have a lot to contribute to the enterprise. Analyzing how one could build a computer program to emulate a human function is a very useful way of enumerating alternative processing modules and algorithms. Not only does this approach raise alternatives that may not have otherwise been considered, but it also eliminates others by forcing one to work them out concretely enough to reveal their flaws (the Guzman approach to vision is a good example; see Winston, 1978).

Limitations and Virtues of the Cognitive Psychology Approach

The predominant approach in cognitive psychology is solidly empirical: researchers have developed methodologies that make use of response times, error rates, and various judgments and have attempted to develop models that account for these data. The methodologies used have become very sophisticated and powerful, allowing researchers to observe quite subtle regularities in processing. As we saw in the previous section, such data place strong constraints on theories of processing: since processing takes place in real time, there will always be measurable consequences of any given sequence of activity.

Although cognitive psychologists occasionally focus on the nature of the step-by-step process a subject is using to carry out an entire task (e.g., see Simon and Simon, 1978), more typically they are interested in studying how information is represented and processed within a single stage of processing. However, it has proven difficult to draw firm conclusions about the representations or processes used in even one stage of processing because of two general problems: structure/process trade-offs and task demand artifacts.

Anderson (1978) demonstrated that structure/process trade-offs are in principle always possible, so that, given any set of data, more than one theory can be formulated to account for the data. That is, what are, in one theory, properties of a given representation operated on by a specific process are, in another theory, properties of a different representation operated on by a different process. For example, consider the memory scanning results described by Sternberg (1969). He asked subjects to hold lists of digits in mind, with lists varying from 1 to 6 in length. Shortly thereafter, a probe digit was presented, and subjects were to decide as quickly as possible whether the probe was a member of the list. The time to make this decision increased linearly with increasing set size (by about 39 ms per additional item). One theory of this result posits that the list of digits (the structure) is held in mind and then scanned serially (the process) when the probe arrives. Alternatively, one could posit an unordered collection (the structure) with each item being compared simultaneously with the probe (the process). In this case, all one needs to do is assume that the comparison process slows down as more things need to be compared, and the two theories will mimic each other. More time is required when more items are on the memorized list to be compared with the probe.

In this example, the two theories seem to account for the data equally well—but they were created entirely ad hoc simply to account for the data. Constraints on the theories are required, a source of motivation for selection of the specific representations and processes. Why should information be represented as an ordered list or as an unordered collection? Why is more time required if one compares more items simultaneously? Computational considerations are one possible source of constraint. However, we saw in the previous section that computational constraints in themselves are not sufficient, and in fact the observation of how the system functions puts constraints on computational theories themselves.

Anderson (1978) drew some very pessimistic conclusions from the possibility of structure/process trade-offs, but others such as Hayes-Roth (1979) and Pylyshyn (1979) were less gloomy. The upshot of the debate seems to be that while it is possible to derive inferences about processing mechanisms from behavioral data, it is very difficult to do so. One argument to be developed here is that psychophysiological data are powerful supplements to the usual behavioral data, and would greatly constrain the use of structure/process trade-offs to develop alternative theories.

Another problem in interpreting behavioral data is the possibility of distorting behavior because of perceived task demands. That is, subjects may respond in a manner congruent with their beliefs concerning acceptable behavior to the task and the situation. If they do so, then data from many studies of, for example, mental imagery may say nothing about the nature of the underlying mechanisms, but may only reflect the subjects' understanding of tasks, knowledge of physics and perception, and ability to regulate their response times.

Although the problem of task demands has been brought to the attention of cognitive psychophysiologists primarily in the literature of mental imagery, it is applicable to many domains in cognitive psychology and, indeed, in other areas of psychology. There is no way to ensure that subjects are not unconsciously producing data in accordance with their tacit knowledge about perception and cognition and their understanding of what the task requires them to do. In contrast, not only do neurological maladies produce behavioral deficits of various types, but often the patients are not aware of the nature of the deficits. Thus, psychophysiological data might profitably supplement the usual cognitive data, if for no reason other than to rule out task demand as a source of explanation. And such data are useful for other purposes, as discussed in the following section.

The Strength of a Combined Approach

Psychophysiological approaches can be used to circumvent some of the difficulties inherent in the traditional measures used by cognitive psychologists, which are based strictly on the observation of overt responses. First, structure/process trade-offs are greatly minimized if neurophysiological data are used. By relating processing to anatomical areas, many of the degrees of freedom are removed from cognitive science theories: in all cases in which a given area is active or damaged, the consequences must be the same. When one has fixed the properties of some area, those properties cannot be changed at whim by a theorist in order to account for new data. Second, difficulties due to task demands are virtually eliminated if brain activation measures are used, because subjects cannot respond to explicit task demands by directly altering the activity of specific regions of the brain. Whereas a person can regulate the time taken to press a button, it is not so easy to regulate intentionally the activity of the right parietal lobe, for example. In addition, psychophysiological measures can be used to monitor on-line and in real time the activity of processing entities that are not directly manifested by overt behavior.

The computational approach, by contrast, especially as constrained by data from cognitive psychology, is useful for generating hypotheses about processing mechanisms. Analyzing the requirements of the task at hand and how one would need to program a computer to perform it is a good way to generate alternative possibilities. In addition, this approach provides a way of testing complex theories by actually building a computer program that emulates cognitive processing (see Newell and Simon, 1972). Precise theories of on-line brain functioning may be so complex that many of a theory's implications will be derived only by using simulation models.

Furthermore, once there are prior reasons for positing a specific modular composition of the system, the standard techniques of cognitive psychology become more powerful. When a module is defined, the number of degrees of freedom is reduced for possible structure/process trade-offs. That is, without modularity constraints, any part of the system can be invoked in combination with any other part to explain a specific result; but if a result can be shown to rest on the operation of a specific module, the explanation of the result is limited to fewer alternatives. When well-specified classes of alternative theories are defined, cognitive psychologists will be better able to specify which phenomena will distinguish among competing accounts (for an example see the mental rotation case noted above in Kosslyn, 1980: Ch.8).

One example of progress following from such a combined approach began with computational analyses suggesting that spatial localization should be decomposed into at least two types of processes. On one hand, if one were to build a machine to recognize semirigid objects (e.g., a human form) it would be desirable to include a module to encode representations of rather broad categories of spatial relations among parts. Such representations would be constant over different contortions of the object. For example, the forearm and upper arm remain connected (a categorical relation) no matter how they are configured. On the other hand, if the machine is also intended to navigate and reach for objects, it is desirable to include a module to encode representations of the specific metric coordinates between parts or objects. For these purposes, a broad category of relations (e.g., one object is "left of" another) is not useful; one needs to know precise positions. The possible distinction between these types of representation has been investigated by noting that categorical representations are language-like (all can be easily named by a word or two) and hence might be processed more effectively in the left cerebral hemisphere. In contrast, coordinate representations are critical for navigation, which appears to draw in large part on right hemisphere processes. And in fact, it has been found that categorical spatial relations are apprehended more effectively in the left hemisphere, whereas coordinate relations are apprehended more effectively in the right hemisphere (Kosslyn, 1987, 1988); this inference is based in part on work using some of the technologies discussed in this report. This dissociation provides evidence for the existence of distinct processes underlying the two types of spatial representation, which was not obvious until computational analyses led to the distinction between the two and specific brain-based hypotheses were tested.

In summary, psychophysiological data offer constraints both on theories of processing modules and theories of the algorithms used. The logic of dissociations and associations in deficits or patterns of brain activation is a powerful way of developing and testing computational theories, particularly so if it is supplemented by the methodologies and analytic techniques of cognitive psychology. The methodologies developed by the cognitive psychologists for the most part can be adapted for use in psychophysiological studies.

3
Four New Technologies: Research Findings

This chapter provides technical discussions of each of the four technologies examined by the committee. Each discussion covers four areas: a brief description, the background of relevant research findings, an assessment of the likelihood that progress will be made, and an outline of opportunities for basic and applied research. Our assessments of the likelihood of progress are based on the most recent developments in empirical research, which are reviewed in varying amounts of detail depending on the field. Implications are drawn from the best experimental work reported to date. Research opportunities are discussed in terms of the conceptual foundations established by the current research and the technological breakthroughs that make possible finer definition of brain functions involved in cognitive processes. One important and general conclusion emerges from these discussions, namely the importance of exploiting the complementary advantages of the different technologies as, for example, employing both PET and MRI methodologies for solving problems of anatomical localization of physiological processes. Progress will depend, however, on solving the problems considered in detail in Chapter 4.

EVENT-RELATED BRAIN POTENTIALS

Event related brain potentials (ERPs) are obtained by placing electrodes on a person's head and recording electroencephalographic (EEG) activity while the subject is engaged in a task. By means of signal averaging it is possible to extract from the EEG (a voltage ×

time function) estimates of the portion of the voltage (the ERP) that is time-locked to events associated with the task. These ERPs represent the synchronized activity of neuronal ensembles whose fields are so aligned that they summate to produce potentials that are large enough to be recorded over the scalp. The ERP consists of a sequence of named components whose amplitude, latency, and scalp distribution vary systematically with the conditions of stimulation, with the subject, and with the processing required by the eliciting events. Variations in the behavior of the components of the ERP can be used in the study of sensory and cognitive function (Callaway, Tueting and Koslow, 1978; Hillyard and Kutas, 1983).

Background of Research Findings

The ERPs provide a rich class of responses that may, within the appropriate research paradigm, allow the study of processes that are not readily accessible to experimental psychologists by other means. The key assumption of cognitive psychophysiology is that ERP components are manifestations at the scalp of the activity of specific intracranial processors. The reference is not to specific neuroanatomical entities, but rather to specific functional processors. While networks of nuclei may be involved in a dynamic fashion in the activity represented by each ERP component, our current understanding of the underlying neuroanatomy is, for most components, insufficient to generate meaningful neuroanatomical hypotheses. But the available data regarding the consistency with which certain components measured at the scalp behave permit us to hypothesize that these components do signal the activation of internal subroutines.

These remarks do not imply that the electrical activity recorded at the scalp is itself of functional significance. For our purposes, the ERPs may be due solely to the fortuitous summation of electrical fields that surround active neurons. Although some have argued that EEG fields do have functional significance (Freeman, 1975), we remain agnostic on this issue. We are not asserting that the ERPs are epiphenomena. Rather, we are saying that from the perspective of the cognitive scientist, it is sufficient to elucidate the functional role, in information-processing terms, of the subroutines manifested by the ERP components.

Once the existence of a component is well established, the essential tools of the cognitive psychophysiological paradigm are used to identify the subroutine it manifests and to articulate its parameters. This search and analysis require that: (1) we elucidate the antecedent conditions under which the component is elicited, from which (2) we derive a model of its subroutine that (3) we test by predicting the consequences of "calling the subroutine" (i.e., of engaging the processes whose activation is manifested at the scalp). With the information thus gained, psychophysiology provides a repertoire of tools, a collection of components, each of which can be used in the appropriate circumstances to augment the armamentarium of the cognitive scientist (Donchin, 1981).

Likelihood That Progress Will be Made

The ensemble of information-processing activities manifested by the ERPs is already quite rich. Additional components are being discovered and deeper understanding is being reached of components that have been known since the 1960s. In principle, all these components can be used in cognitive psychophysiology. A good start has been made and, as is made clear in subsequent pages, the area is rich in promise and substantive progress.

The following paragraphs list some of the components that have attracted the most substantial investigative efforts. Components are labeled as <N>egative or <P>ositive to indicate the direction of the voltage change from the base line. The number following the character refers to the modal latency, in milliseconds (msec), of the component, measured from the onset of the precipitating event.

N100—Direction of Attention

Hillyard and his associates have shown that the N100 component is affected by the directions of the subject's attention. Events in the focus of attention tend to elicit a somewhat larger N100. The effect is reliable and can be used to monitor changes in the direction of attention or changes in the attentional level. Thus, the N100 can play a role either in ascertaining whether the subject is actually following instructions with regard to the allocation of attention or in determining whether events in the environment have caused the subject to shift attention. Research on the behavioral correlates of N100, and other negative components, is a very active field of investigation. There is considerable interest in resolving the many different negative components that appear in the first 200 msec following the eliciting event and in elucidating their functional significance (for reviews see Naatanen and Picton, 1987, and Hillyard and Hansen, 1986). There is an active examination of the differences and similarities in the nature of selective attention in different sensory modalities. Furthermore, extensive work that illuminates central issues in the theory of attention is being done (Hillyard and Hansen, 1986).

N200—Detection of Mismatch

Considerable evidence exists that the N200 is elicited by events that violate a subject's expectations, even if they occur outside the focus of attention. Thus, the N200 seems to be a manifestation of the activation of a mismatch detector. This component seems to be the least susceptible to control by the subject's voluntary actions. The occurrence of any deviation from regularity, indeed any mismatch between an event and its immediate predecessor, elicits an N200. Examination of these components continues and is being extended to fairly abstract information-processing activities. Thus, for example, there is considerable interest in the role that these negative components play in studies of lexical decision (Naatanen, 1982).

P300—A Manifestation of Strategic Processing

When subjects are presented with events that are both task relevant and rare, a prominent positive component with a latency of at least 300 msec is elicited. The literature concerned with the P300 is quite extensive (see Donchin et al., 1986; Pritchard, 1981; and Rossler, 1983, for reviews). Johnson (1988, in press) has summarized much of the evidence concerning its antecedent conditions and has concluded that the elicitation and amplitude of the P300 depends on a multiplicative relationship between the subjective probability of events (the rarer the event, the larger the P300) and the amount of information and the utility of the information to the subject (the more information, the larger the elicited P300). Donchin and his colleagues have interpreted these data within the context of a model that assumes that the P300 is a manifestation of the revision of mental models (see Donchin and Coles, in press; Donchin, 1981). Much empirical evidence supports a wide variety of applications of the P300, including the measurement of mental workload (Gopher and Donchin, 1986; Donchin et al., 1986), analyses of memory mechanisms (Neville et al., 1986; Karis, Fabiani, and Donchin, 1984), and concession making in bargaining situations (Druckman, Karis, and Donchin, 1983; Karis, Druckman, Lissak, and Donchin, 1984). The latency of the P300 has also proven to be of use. It can be shown to be relatively independent of response execution processes and can thus serve as a pure measure of mental timing (Kutas, McCarthy, and Donchin, 1977; McCarthy and Donchin, 1983).

N400—Semantic Mismatch

Kutas and Hillyard (1980, 1984) have shown that words that are in some way incongruous or unexpected in a semantic sense within a discourse elicit an ERP component that is negative and has a latency of about 400 msec (see Kutas and Van Petten, 1987, for a review). Kutas and her coworkers have subsequently shown that the amplitude of the N400 is inversely proportional to the degree to which the context constrains the word eliciting the N400. The measurement of N400 makes it possible to address unresolved issues in psycholinguistics. Thus, for example, Van Petten and Kutas (1987) show rather persuasively that they can measure the degree to which sentences impose constraints on their constituent words by examining the N400 elicited by these words. This application of N400 in psycholinguistics is increasingly active (Fischler et al., 1983, 1985, 1987).

The Readiness Potential and the Contingent Negative Variation—Preparation to Respond

Kornhuber and Deecke (1965) have shown that voluntary responses are preceded by a slow negative wave, which they labeled the readiness potential (RP). Walter and his colleagues (1964) have demonstrated that a slow negative wave develops between a first stimulus, which heralds the later arrival of a second stimulus, to which the subject must respond. They called this wave the contingent negative variation (CNV). (Note the different labeling systems.) As on a map of lower Manhattan, the orderly system of letters and numbers used to label the faster components gives way to a system in which each component carries a name given it by its discoverer. The RP and the CNV are among several ERP components that are called event-preceding negativities. They are quite clearly related to the activation of preparatory, often unconscious, processes by the subject. Their usefulness in the study of cognitive processes is extensive. For example, Coles and his colleagues (1985) have shown that it is possible to determine, from the extent to which these potentials are larger over one hemisphere than the other, which response the subject was contemplating regardless of the response that has actually been made.

Opportunities for Basic and Applied Research

It is not possible in this brief review to do justice to so active a research enterprise. The work reviewed above refers to some of the well-established research activities. It may be useful, however, to note a number of developing research areas that are likely to play a central role in the coming decade.

One of the more significant efforts is the increasing practicality of elucidating the intracranial origin of the components. We referred elsewhere to this work, but it is important to underline the fact that much of the technological and conceptual development required has become readily available only very recently. Several laboratories had access to patients with indwelling electrodes from the earliest days of ERP research. However, only within the last decade has it become possible to deal with the massive data base generated in such studies. Furthermore, there are significant developments in the theoretical understanding of the nature of the models needed to relate intracranial activity to scalp recorded activity (see, for example, Scherg and Von Carmon, 1985; Nunez, 1981). There also is an increasing number of investigations of analogous processes in nonhuman species (Deadwyler et al., 1985; Arthur and Starr, 1984). The work in humans using indwelling electrodes, neuromagnetic recording, and clinical observations on the effects of lesions (Johnson and Fedio, 1986) is likely to combine in the near future with the work in animals to yield much deeper understanding of the neurophysiological basis of the ERPs.

The development of display methodology is likely to affect progress in the field, as noted below. It is largely the case that investigators are forced to select a very small portion of their data for display and analysis. The number of waveforms analyzed is generally much smaller than can be easily acquired, and the number of measurements made on these waveforms is also rather small. The ability to summarize and combine much larger masses of data provided by mapping approaches is likely to transform the field. However, this will be true only if the summaries and the displays are guided by proper statistical and substantive theories. It is to this area of research that much attention needs to be paid in the near term (see, for example, Skrandies and Lehman, 1982).

Much work in cognitive psychophysiology is motivated by applied interests. The use of ERPs recorded from the brainstem is routine in neurology and audiology, as are various diagnostic procedures that measure the speed of neuronal conduction in the response of various systems to changes in steady-state stimuli. More controversial at this time are applications of some of the components in the diagnosis of neurological and psychiatric disorders. There is extensive interest in a report (Goodin, Squires, and Starr, 1978) that interpretation of the latency of the P300 may allow a diagnosis of either dementia or depression. Begleiter and his associates (1984) have been applying ERP measures in studies of the familial risk for alcoholism.

In addition to the clinical work, there is active interest in the feasibility of using ERPs and other psychophysiological measures in the field known as engineering psychology. *Human Factors*, the official journal of the Human Factors Society, devoted a special issue (Kramer, 1987) to examine psychophysiological measures. The usefulness of the P300 as a measure of mental workload has been examined in some detail by Donchin and his colleagues (see Gopher and Donchin, 1986, for a review). The work is continuing and diversifying.

Methodological Issues

Data acquisition is not a source of serious problems in ERP research, depending as it does on established technologies. However, experimental design, measurement, and data analysis present serious challenges that require attention. We briefly discuss three parts of the methodology: recording techniques, data analysis, and display methodologies.

The technology required for recording ERPs is largely mature. It is identical to that required for recording the EEG. The EEG is digitized, either on-line or off-line, and the ERP, whose amplitude ranges between 5 and 10 microvolts, is extracted by signal averaging. This well-established procedure capitalizes on the fact that the part of the signal that is time-locked to events has a constant time course following the event while all other activity follows a randomly varying time course.

The data base acquired in ERP experiments does present formidable problems of analysis. Typically, 5 to 10 subjects are run, each in several sessions. In each session, data may be acquired for 5 to 10 separate conditions, where each condition requires the presentation of 30 to 200 repetitions of the same stimulus. For each presentation, the EEG from 5 to 32 recording channels is digitized over an epoch lasting as long as 2 to 3 seconds at the digitizing rate of 100 to 500 samples per second.

All these data are typically stored on magnetic tape. Full storage of single trial data is preferable, especially in studies of cognitive function, because it has proven useful to consider the subject's actual performance on each trial in extracting the ERPs. Thus, for example, it may be of interest to examine separately trials on which the subject's response was fast and those on which the response was slow. Such selective averaging is one of the most powerful tools available to the cognitive psychophysiologist. Note that saving of the single trials allows the use of off-line filtering of artifacts. This strategy prevents the loss of trials. Currently available procedures render obsolete any study in which a substantial percentage of the data is rejected. In any event, even when just the average ERPs are retained, the analytical tasks are formidable. An extensive literature beyond the scope of this report is concerned with these issues (see Coles et al., 1986, for a review).

Even though considerable sophistication is invested in the analysis of data obtained in ERP experiments, the visual inspection of the data remains critically important. It would be rare for a study of ERPs to be published without a visual display of the waveforms. The mere tabulation of measures and the associated statistical tests would be considered inadequate, as they do not allow an evaluation of the quality of recordings. In the past, data were presented largely in the form of plots of voltage changes as a function of time, one plot for each electrode site; this remains the modality of choice. However, the reduced cost of computing power and the increased sophistication of graphic display devices triggered the emergence of displays that map the variations of the voltage over the head at successive instants in time. These "brain maps" represent the changing pattern of activity at varying points in time in a two-dimensional and easily visualizable display. However, all the mapping techniques discussed in this report, including brain mapping, would greatly benefit from an effort to develop statistical methods that can cope with this complex data base.

NEUROMAGNETISM: THE MAGNETOENCEPHALOGRAM

The term *neuromagnetism* refers to the study of the magnetic fields that accompany the flow of ionic currents inside neurons, as opposed to the flow of current within the overall volume of the cranial contents. Neuromagnetic methods are employed in the study of extracranial magnetic fields. By analogy with electroencephalography, which involves the study of electrical *potential* differences between electrodes attached to the scalp, *magnetoencephalography* (MEG) is now the standard term used to refer to the study of the brain's varying *magnetic* field. In addiiton, by analogy with ERPs, extracranial magnetic fields that are time-locked to physical stimuli (e.g., changes in visual patterns, noise bursts) are referred to as event-related fields (ERFs). As in the study of evoked potentials, it is customary to distinguish between steady states and transient responses, except that the measures used are time-varying amplitudes of neuromagnetic fields rather than of voltages.

Background of Research Findings

The first systematic studies of neuromagnetism appeared in 1975. At first, they took the form of demonstrating that it was possible to detect visually evoked fields. These were rapidly followed by the demonstration that fields also could be evoked by auditory and somatosensory stimuli, and that fields systematically preceded the occurrence of simple motor acts. In 1975, a singularly interesting finding was reported: it was found that the amplitude of the field associated with stimulation of the little finger had a different distribution on the scalp than that associated with stimulation of the thumb (Brenner, Williamson, and Kaufman, 1975). This led almost immediately to the notion that the mapped field could be compared with that which would be produced by an equivalent current dipole source, and the source could be located within the three-dimensional volume of the brain.

The magnetic field is associated with the intracellular currents of a limited population of neurons in the brain. The field produced by these neurons is essentially indistinguishable from that which would be produced by an arbitrarily small segment of current. This small segment is commonly referred to as a current dipole.

Various groups began to use this approach, which entailed taking sequential measurements from many places on the head. Since the only available instrument at that time incorporated a single superconducting quantum interference device (SQUID) and sensing coil, the task proved to be very laborious and subject to errors in positioning the sensing coil over the head. It quickly became apparent that multiple sensors would be necessary to realize the full potential of the technique. The main advantage of magnetic recording is that, using a minimum number of assumptions, it is possible to determine the three-dimensional location, geometric orientation, and strength of equivalent current dipole sources. This advantage makes it possible to distinguish between changes in field intensity due to a change in amount of neural activity resulting from an experimental manipulation and changes in source location and orientation. Multiple sensors are needed for this purpose.

The group at the Helsinki Technological University was the first to construct a multichannel system. This included four SQUIDs and four sensing coils. Owing to a specific feature of the Finnish design, one of the four channels was never used in the many useful experiments conducted by that group (Hari et al., 1982, 1984); their system was functionally a three-channel system.

At about the same time, the group at New York University collaborated with the S.H.E. Corp. of San Diego (now Biomagnetic Technologies, Inc.) in designing and developing a five-channel system that incorporated the newer and more sensitive dc SQUIDs. Actually, nine SQUIDs were used: five were used for sensing the brain's field; three were used for monitoring the field in the x, y, and z axes; and one was used for monitoring the spatial gradient of the field along the z axis of the dewar. In effect, these channels were used to monitor the ambient field. Their gains were empirically adjusted and their outputs subtracted from those of the signal channels to reduce the effect of this ambient noise. This was the first system to employ electronic noise cancellation techniques. It was introduced into the laboratory in 1983 and proved extremely effective, even in the absence of shielding, in making measurements more quickly and accurately than was possible previously.

Based on their experience in constructing a five-channel system, Biomagnetic Technologies, Inc., went on to develop a similar seven-channel system. Such systems are now installed at New York University, the National Institutes of Health, Vanderbilt University, the Scripps Clinic in La Jolla, the Los Alamos National Laboratory, the Free University in West Berlin, the University of Texas School of Medicine in Galveston, and at Henry Ford Hospital in Detroit and in other laboratories in Europe. In some cases two such instruments are present in the same laboratory, thus providing a total of 14 sensing channels for concurrent use. CTF, a Vancouver based company, manufactured a single-channel system that is in use at Simon Frazer University and at the University of Wisconsin. It should be noted that only three laboratories are devoting a substantial effort to the study of cognitive processes, the rest focusing on clinical problems.

Likelihood That Progress Will Be Made

All this ferment in the development of the technology of neuromagnetism is undoubtedly related to the very strong claims made on its behalf. The strongest of these claims is related to the presumption that the extracellular volume currents that underlie the EEG and the ERP do not contribute substantially to the magnetic field. Furthermore, the neuromagnetic and electrical methods yield different and complementary results. Since the distribution of intracranial volume currents is strongly influenced by features of the skull such as the orbits of the eyes, the sutures in the skull, and other anisotropies of conductivity, source localization using simple concentric sphere models should be subject to considerable error. If it is true that these same conditions have little effect on the extracranial magnetic field, then relatively simple models of the head should permit excellent source localization. One strong claim is that it is possible to locate intracranial sources of neuromagnetic fields with a precision that is not possible when using similar electrical measurements. To the extent that investigators find it important that activity of particular portions of the brain be identified with processes underlying cognition, this attribute of neuromagnetism may be of great value. There are empirical bases for this strong claim that we review below.

One of the more impressive experiments, demonstrating the ability of neuromagnetic methods to resolve sources, described the tonotopic organization of a portion of the human auditory cortex (Romani, Williamson, and Kaufman, 1982). Tone stimuli of different frequencies were modulated by a 32 Hz sinusoid. The steady-state evoked field at the frequency of the modulating sinusoid was measured at many places on the side of the head. All the carrier frequencies were presented at each position of the single-channel sensor; the sensor was then moved and the responses measured again at another position. After the experiment was completed, all the averaged responses associated with each carrier frequency were collected and used to generate isofield contour plots. These plots revealed a very precise linear relationship between distance along the cortex and the logarithm of the frequency of the carrier. This log-linear relationship proved that an equal number of neurons was dedicated to each octave of the acoustic spectrum that was studied. Furthermore, the "sources" responding to each of the carrier frequencies were as close as 2 mm to each other. In addition, the current dipole moment that would produce the measured fields was consistent with that which would be produced if as few as 10,000 neurons contributed to it.

Using the methods described previously, other studies describe results that are almost as spectacular. For example, Hari et al. (1982) showed that the magnetic counterpart to ERP component N100, elicited by auditory stimuli, has at least one major source in the auditory cortex itself. Pellizone et al. (1985) demonstrated that the sources of N100 and P200 have spatially separated sources in auditory cortex. Hoke et al. (1988) demonstrated that there are multiple sources for N100, and these are tonotopically organized just as is the different region of auditory cortex studied by Romani et al. (1982). Okada, Kaufman, and Williamson (1982) resolved separate sources along the somatosensory cortex representing the little finger, index finger, thumb, and ankle. Hari et al. (1984) demonstrated the existence of a secondary somatosensory cortex in humans. Such findings lend credence to the strong claim that the skull and other tissues are essentially transparent to magnetic fields at the frequencies of interest, and measuring these fields avoids some of the problems associated with effects of conductivity differences on the flow of volume currents.

Although empirical data such as these are impressive, they do not provide a direct validation of the strong claim regarding source localization. This issue has been addressed in a few cases. Barth et al. (1986) placed a physical current dipole inside the skull of a cadaver filled with a conducting gel. Using various models of the skull, he predicted the field pattern that would be observed at the surface of the skull. The error of computed source position, as determined from X-rays of the skull, was on the order of 2 or 3 mm for sources 2-3 cm deep, but grew to as much as 8 mm for sources as deep as 5 cm. The error was greatest in the temporal region, and least in the more spherical occipital region. (These errors could easily be reduced by using a more appropriate model, e.g., one using a sphere that best fits the local interior curvature of the skull, or perhaps a model using the actual skull shape.) Impressive results concerning the field distribution were obtained when the skull was altered. In one case, a large aperture was cut into the skull. This would drastically alter the distribution of volume currents. However, the observed field pattern was essentially unaltered. The same was true when the aperture was filled with a balloon having a very different conductivity compared with the conducting gel. Such insensitivity to radical changes in the distribution of volume currents is rather strong evidence that the claims are valid.

This evidence is also consistent with excellent results reported by Chapman (1983), Ricci et al. (1985), and Barth et al. (1984, 1986) in locating epileptic foci. In some cases these were located at positions that corresponded rather precisely to the centers of gravity of tumors that could be visualized by means of CT (X-ray computed tomography) scans. In other cases, surgical verification of location was provided by the finding of millimeter-sized tumors at about the positions at which field mapping indicated they should be. It may also be worth noting that MRI (magnetic resonance imaging) scans of one of the subjects used in the experiment by Romani et al. (1982) revealed that the source of activity evoked by acoustic stimuli was deep within and on the floor of the lateral sulcus. Finally, Okada and Nicholson (1988; see also Okada, Lauritzen, and Nicholson, 1987), using the turtle brain in vitro, located 1 cubic mm of active tissue with an accuracy of 1 mm, from field measurements made at a distance of 2 cm, despite the presence of widespread volume currents in the conducting solution in which the turtle brain was immersed.

By contrast with the extensive ERP and EEG literatures, investigation of the ERF and of the MEG as it relates to cognitive processes has a short history. One contribution of some importance is the study of the effect of selective attention on the amplitude of the magnetic N100 (Curtis, Kaufman, and Williamson, 1988).

It is well established that the amplitude of the auditory ERP ranging from about 40 msec to more than 200 msec after stimulation is enhanced by attending to the stimulus. This time interval includes the classic N100 and P200 components of the ERP. The extensive literature in this area is reviewed by Naatanen and Picton (1987), who consider the work of Hillyard and his colleagues in some detail. It is generally agreed by these authors that a low-frequency negative component that overlaps the N100 in time, sometimes referred to as the negativity difference wave, is also affected by attending. In fact, it has been suggested that the change in amplitude of the N100 with attention may be largely due to a shift in amplitude of other components, including but not limited to the negativity difference wave, that overlap the N100 in time. Naatanen and Picton present evidence suggesting that there are as many as six different components, each with a source in a different portion of the brain, that contribute to the attention effect, and that the source of the N100 apparently lying in or near auditory cortex may actually contribute little to it. Even so, the fact that the effect of selective attending may be displayed as early as 40 msec after stimulus presentation is taken by Hillyard as being consistent with the early filter model of attention proposed by Treisman (1969).

The experiment by Curtis et al. (1988) employed a dichotic listening paradigm similar in many respects to that of Hillyard and colleagues. The outputs of the neuromagnetometer were bandpassed between 1 and 40 Hz so that the low frequencies that contribute to the negativity difference wave could not contribute to any effect of attention on the magnetic counterparts of the N100 and the P200. Despite this, the amplitudes of these components when the stimuli were attended to were almost twice that of the same components when the stimuli were ignored. Furthermore, there was no sign of activity from any other sources such as the frontal lobes. The equivalent current dipole sources of the magnetic N100 and P200 were located in or near the auditory cortex. Since the region of the brain from which the magnetic N100 appears to emanate is tonotopically organized (Hoke et al., 1988), it appears that attention serves to modulate the activity of small populations of neurons early in the processing chain. However, since the effects of attention were observed in averaged responses, it is conceivable that efferents from later stages of processing provide feedback after the first few stimulus presentations, and these efferents affect the response magnitude of neurons at the sources of the N100. Therefore, we cannot rule out either a filter at a later stage of processing (as in the theory of Deutsch and Deutsch, 1963) or some other process similar to that described by Neisser (1967) or by Hochberg (1968). Clearly, experiments should be conducted to determine whether other later stages of processing are part of a feedback loop. The conduct of such experiments will depend on the use of large arrays of sensors, as they will be required for monitoring brain activity from many different places at the same time.

It has been shown experimentally that it is possible to detect a magnetic counterpart to a negativity difference wave in auditory responses to novel stimuli. This wave is probably related to the negativity that was described by Hillyard et al. (1973), and its magnetic counterpart appears also to have its source near auditory cortex.

Still another contribution of ERF studies is the first report that the equivalent current dipole source of the P300 is in or near the hippocampal formation (Okada, Kaufman, and Williamson, 1982). This finding is consistent with data obtained using indwelling electrodes in epileptics. But electrical studies in which patients having unilateral temporal lobectomies show no shift in the distribution of the P300, and studies involving animal models show results that in some cases are inconsistent with this interpretation and consistent with those of other studies (e.g., Buchwald, 1987). These inconsistencies remain to be resolved.

The literature concerning the relationship between neuromagnetism and cognition is quite slender. As stated earlier, until now the main focus of basic research has been on sensory processes. There are currently several major efforts getting under way that are designed to test the usefulness of neuromagnetism in medical practice, and three laboratories are currently investigating neural processes involved in cognitive processes. Publications should be imminent.

While little has been accomplished in directly contributing to cognitive neuroscience, it is clear that the necessary foundations for future progress have been laid. The emergence of multiple sensor neuromagnetometers and of theory and algorithms that allow the processing of data from many such channels is particularly important. It has led to a growing awareness that source localization and resolution are possible only when an adequate number of sensors is used, whether these be magnetic field sensors or electrodes. At the present time it is possible to study the activity of limited regions of the brain and how this activity is affected by factors such as cognitive load or changes in perception. It seems likely that many studies will employ the paradigms already used with so much success in ERP research in an effort to determine which parts of the brain are actually involved. This modest approach promises to be useful in that it will enable ERP researchers to determine if a given component they observe is attributable to a single source or to several widely separated sources whose activity overlaps in time. Such efforts will undoubtedly sharpen the skills of workers in neuromagnetism, and they will ultimately result in branching out to develop paradigms that are uniquely suited to their own methodology.

Opportunities for Basic and Applied Research

Several problems associated with the interpretation of ERP results can now be addressed. These include deciding whether the N100 and P200 are attributable to multiple sources and the degree to which the variance in the electrical P300 can be accounted for by changes in the magnetic P300. Such studies will require the joint use of ERP and ERF techniques. The urgent need for concurrent recording of electrical and magnetic data cannot be overstated. Unless precise and quantitative procedures are employed, it will not be possible to determine the degree to which one of these measurement modalities reveals information that cannot be obtained by means of the other modality.

Among the most promising future developments is the advent of truly large arrays of neuromagnetic sensors. The study of correlated activity among all of these sensors will make it possible to examine the waxing and waning of activity of multiple sources in the spontaneous MEG and also when specific event-related tasks are performed. The complex chains of events occurring at many places within the brain during high-level tasks, e.g., retrieving memories, engaging in speech production, perceiving stereoscopic depth, etc., are very difficult to study with existing instruments. Current topographical EEG studies are essentially two dimensional, and the locations of the sources of the potentials cannot be estimated accurately, even with the use of 30 to 60 electrodes. The promise of this approach can best be realized using large arrays of sensors and analytical tools that will reveal the changes that occur over time in brain activity within a three-dimensional volume. In principle, there is no technical reason why this cannot be achieved, especially if complementary technologies are brought to bear on the problem of how to constrain solutions to the inverse problem, discussed in Chapter 4.

As we have already stressed, there are some inherent ambiguities in interpreting neuromagnetic measures. It is not known whether there is a flow of current in opposed directions at the same time in many portions of the cortex. If this is a significant occurrence, then it leaves us with an apparently weak response although the underlying activity is in fact very strong. Animal models and methods of current source density analysis applied to their exposed brains should help to clarify this issue. So too would correlated brain imaging studies (see the next section). These, however, should not be mere replications of experiments across different populations of subjects; they should involve the same subjects and the experimenters should have the broad biophysical skills needed to interpret such data. In this same connection, it may be instructive to conduct studies involving clinical populations, including patients with split brains, so that it becomes relatively easy to isolate anatomically symmetrical regions from each other. Thus, the use of both electrical and magnetic measures in split brain patients (and of the many techniques developed to study such patients) can lead to very suggestive results.

IMAGING TECHNIQUES I: POSITRON EMISSION TOMOGRAPHY

Positron emission tomography (PET) is a nuclear medicine technique that produces an image of the distribution of a previously administered radioactively labeled compound in any desired section of the body (Raichle, 1983). Radioactive labeling is the chemical synthesis of a compound in which one of the atoms is radioactive. PET images are highly faithful representations of the spatial distribution of these radioactively labeled compounds at selected planes through the tissue. These images reflect the behavior of the particular compound that has been labeled. A wide variety of compounds have been labeled permitting measurements of local blood flow, metabolism, and chemistry.

Background of Research Findings

Using ^{18}F-labeled fluoro-deoxyglucose, PET investigators (Phelps et al., 1979; Reivich et al., 1979) quickly adapted the successful deoxyglucose autoradiographic technique (Sokoloff et al., 1977) for measuring local brain glucose metabolism. PET tended to become synonymous with deoxyglucose measurements of local brain glucose metabolism in humans. Many attractive, color-coded images of normal as well as diseased human brains at work soon appeared in the scientific literature, at scientific meetings, and even in the media. What escaped the notice of many was that PET employs a variety of quantitative tracer techniques. Each of these techniques uses a different mathematical model and a different radio-labeled compound. These techniques can now be used to make measurements of many different variables, such as local blood flow (Raichle et al., 1983), blood volume (Martin, Powers, and Raichle, 1987), oxygen consumption (Mintun et al., 1984), pH (Brooks et al., 1984), permeability (Herscovitch et al., 1987), receptor binding (Perlmutter et al.,

1986) and transmitter metabolism (Garnett, Firnau, and Nahmias, 1983). It can be anticipated that additional PET techniques will be developed in response to new and important biological questions that justify the time (often 2 to 5 years) and expense required to develop the relevant radio-pharmaceuticals and tracer strategy.

Likelihood That Progress Will Be Made

The capacity of PET to contribute to a better understanding of brain function has been demonstrated. Abundant evidence indicates that functional activity, such as somaesthesis, audition, movements of all types, vision, and language, cause striking changes in local brain blood flow and glucose uptake, which can be quite dramatically demonstrated with PET (Raichle, 1987). Analysis of such images has progressed from simple qualitative, uncontrolled demonstrations of anticipated changes to more sophisticated studies using rigorously controlled experimental paradigms and precise analytical techniques (Petersen et al., 1988).

In the studies by Petersen et al. the objective was to use PET measurements of blood flow to locate the regions of the human cerebral cortex concerned with the elementary mental operations of visual and auditory word processing. Four behavioral conditions formed a three-level subtractive hierarchy: passively viewing a cross hairs on a television monitor; passively viewing or hearing single words at one per second; repeating the words; and generating a use for the words. Each task state was assumed to add a single process to those of its subordinate control state. Direct evidence to support this assumption is in press (Petersen et al., 1988). Because of the short measurement time and the repeatability of the measurement, all tasks were performed by each subject in the study. The first-level comparison, the presentation of single words without a lexical task, was compared with visual fixation without word presentation. No motor output nor volitional lexical processing was required in this task; rather simple sensory input and involuntary word-form processing were targeted by this subtraction. In the second-level comparison, speaking each presented word was compared with word presentation without speech. Areas involved in output coding and motor control were targeted by this comparison. In the third-level comparison, saying a use for each presented word (e.g., if "cake" was presented, to say "eat"), was compared with speaking presented words. This comparison targeted areas involved in the task of semantic processing (verb-noun association) as distinguished from speech, sensory input, and involuntary word-form processing.

Images were analyzed by paired intrasubject subtraction. Task-state minus control-state subtractions created images of the regional blood flow changes associated with the operations of each cognitive level. Intersubject averaging was used to increase the signal-to-noise ratio of these subtracted images.

The results of this complex study provide evidence for multiple, parallel routes between localized sensory-specific, phonological, articulatory, and semantic coding areas. More important, this study may be a prime example of what is required to make effective use of PET in cognitive psychophysiology. The study combined state-of-the-art PET techniques with sophisticated stimulation paradigms; it arose from close collaboration among investigators with expertise in PET, human neurobiology, and cognitive neuropsychology. The study seems to provide unique new insights into the functional anatomy of perception, motor control, and language.

It should be clear from the above material that PET will play a significant role in understanding the function of the human brain.

Opportunities for Basic and Applied Research

It may be argued by some that despite the developments described in this report, it is virtually impossible for PET to reveal the underlying *neuronal* events participating in such changes (e.g., blood flow and volume or transmitter metabolism), and hence it can contribute little to our understanding of how the brain works. However, it seems fair to assume that once PET has safely identified a specific area of normal human or primate cortex involved in a well-defined type of information processing (a task it is uniquely equipped to do), other neurobiological techniques can be brought to bear on the exact nature of the process. Complementary interaction of this type between cognitive psychophysiology and neurobiology can serve to further our understanding of the human brain.

IMAGING TECHNIQUES II: MAGNETIC RESONANCE IMAGING

Magnetic resonance imaging (MRI) is based on the fact that some atomic nuclei act like tiny bar magnets when placed in a magnetic field. When they are aligned in a magnetic field they can be excited in controlled ways by irradiation with radio frequency energy. During recovery from such manipulations, these tiny bar magnets or dipoles emit radio frequency signals that contain a great deal of information about their chemical environment. Depending on the strength of such signals, images of sections of the body can be obtained with this technique. From such images one can obtain quantitiative information about tissue biochemistry, acidity, and metabolism as well as anatomy.

Background of Research Findings

Abundant evidence now supports the use of proton MRI in clinical medicine as an excellent way to obtain anatomical information of the human brain in vivo. In many respects, the images are superior to those produced by X-ray computed tomography (CT). The primary contribution of proton MRI to neurobiology will be similar to that of CT, providing accurate information for correlations between specific lesions and the signs and symptoms of illness.

Many nuclei other than hydrogen can be studied with MRI. Of the biologically important ones, ^{31}P, ^{23}Na, and ^{13}C have received the most attention. In a recent review of in vivo spectroscopy techniques (now often referred to as MRS or magnetic resonance spectroscopy) using these nuclei, Prichard and Schulman (1986) have provided exciting new data from an increasing number of studies showing that it is feasible to measure brain ATP, PCr, Pi, and intracellular pH in vivo with phosphorous MRI. Using refined techniques for the hydrogen nuclei, it is possible to measure brain lactate concentrations in humans and a variety of amino acids in animals. Techniques still under development with ^{13}C MRI suggest that it may be possible to monitor a number of specific biochemical reactions in vivo with MRI spectroscopy.

Likelihood That Progress Will Be Made and Opportunities for Research

MRI has played a role almost identical to that of X-ray computed tomography in providing ever more refined anatomical images of the living human brain. This permits detailed clinical-anatomical correlations. Because of its lack of temporal resolution, however, MRI will not replace PET in the area of functional brain mapping.

Because of the exquisite anatomical detail provided by MRI proton images, this technique will probably become the technique of choice for detailed clinical-anatomical correlations. In addition, one can anticipate that MRI proton images will also be used to anatomically constrain PET images with their somewhat poorer anatomical resolution. Thus, brain edges and ventricles can be identified and radioactive counting data blurred into these regions on PET moved back into the brain. Such interaction will require PET and MRI scans in each subject with proper alignment of the planes of section. This will be both expensive and time-consuming; however, at least in selected cases (e.g., cases of aging and dementia with brain atrophy), such an interaction will be essential. More speculative will be the use of MRI to further constrain PET data by defining gray-white matter differences.

COGNITIVE CONSEQUENCES OF BRAIN DAMAGE OR ALTERATIONS

This approach allows for insights into the functioning of the normal human brain. Dissociations, disabilities, and other phenomena instruct the student of cognition at two levels. First, studies on brain-damaged patients are suggestive of the functional architecture of cognition. Second, with the advent of new brain imaging techniques, these same studies can also be suggestive of the brain areas involved with particular functions. This is true not only for cases of hemispheric disconnection but also for the correct characterization of patients with focal brain damage (Jouandet et al., 1987, 1988).

Background of Research Findings

There are two main views on how brain-damaged patients can be used to study cognitive processes. The first assumes that psychological processes are localized in discrete brain areas and that damage to these areas will provoke discrete psychological disturbances. In terms of the doctrine of modularity in cognitive science, the approach hopes to identify brain areas that subserve particular functions as specified in perceptual and cognitive models. With the proliferation of models that become more complex in terms of the processes and subprocesses that are active in perceptual and cognitive processes, the hope has been that new and better brain imaging techniques will assist in a finer-grained identification of the brain areas involved in cognitive and perceptual activities. This position has traditionally not entertained the view that focal brain damage may reveal deficits that are part of a larger process. It has maintained that discrete deficits following prescribed lesions are managed by the brain site in question. This limitation has given rise to an alternative view of how to gain knowledge about cognition from "broken brains."

The second view holds that, since psychological or cognitive processes are widely distributed throughout neural networks, both focal and diffuse brain damage can reveal clues only to the functional structure of cognitive processes; direct clues to brain correlates of cognitive processes are not revealed. The idea here is that cognitive processes are generated by interactions of neural systems that are widely distributed in the brain, and that damage to one area affects other areas. This makes it difficult to ascertain which brain area actually controls a particular function. Yet what is learned, by deduction, is how the cognitive system is structured given how it works in physical disrepair.

The brain lesion approach has yielded some of the most seminal and basic observations to date about brain function. In animal research, many of the major functional areas of the brain have been described (Mishkin, 1982). In humans, the clinical cases have offered major insights into the mechanisms of memory (Milner, 1970; Squire, 1987), perception (Weiskrantz et al., 1974; Holtzman, 1984), attention (Hillyard and Picton, 1987), language (Zurif and Caramazza, 1976), and cerebral lateral specialization (Gazzaniga and Sperry, 1967), to mention a few areas. It was the work on humans, for example, that first implicated the hippocampus in memory mechanisms and gave the first physical evidence that the distinctions between short- and long-term memory were useful for both the brain and psychological sciences. Recent work by Posner has underlined how attentional processes, viewed through cases of brain damage, can be thought of as working independently of other mental structures and yet contributing to most of them. Work on aphasia has made important distinctions about the structure of language, suggesting that different brain areas contribute to syntax as opposed to semantics. The split-brain work that emphasizes the separate capacities of each half brain has now shown how dominant the left brain is for most computational skills, including thinking (Gazzaniga, 1985), imagery (Kosslyn et al., 1985), and belief generation (Gazzaniga, 1985). Finally, work on perceptual processes has continued to identify discrete brain areas associated with particular properties of the visual system such as color and motion detection.

Likelihood That Progress Will Be Made

In the continuing effort to bring greater and greater specificity to structure-function correlates, studying the partially disconnected human brain has been illuminating. Now, using MRI in cases of inadvertent sparing, during brain surgery, of the major fiber pathway in the brain (the corpus callosum), it has been possible to make an exact identification of what the small and discrete fiber systems transmit that is of psychological interest (Gazzaniga et al., 1985). Using this approach, the high degree of specificity of this fiber system for perceptual and cognitive functions is now being demonstrated. The use of MRI for categorizing cortical brain lesions is just beginning (as noted in the previous section).

The localization of function in the human brain has been one of the great classical themes in neurology since at least the time of Paul Broca (1861). Since then, many authors have attempted to correlate various sensory, motor, language, and other higher associational functions to various cortical structures. These results have helped to delineate the functional territories of the human cerebral cortex (Jackson, 1864; Gudden, 1870; Fritsch and Hitzig, 1870; Wernicke, 1864; Dusser de Barrenne, 1916; Cushing, 1932; Gazzaniga and Sperry, 1967).

Today, many workers in this field seem uncomfortable with the functional maps of the human cortex as they now stand: these maps appear insufficiently differentiated, whereas more accurate maps would reveal highly specialized functional processes correlated to highly circumscribed zones in the cortical mantle.

Over the last century, there have been three major obstacles to the development of more highly differentiated functional maps of the human cortex. First, the field of experimental cognitive psychology has had to grow in sophistication; it has and no longer poses an obstacle. But cognitive dysfunction still had to be correlated with some localized cortical damage. This was difficult to do in the days before CT and MRI; then it was necessary either to do a craniotomy or to wait for the final pathology report in order to localize a cortical lesion independently of signs and symptoms. The development of CT and MRI, which precisely and immediately identify the anatomical locations and extents of intracerebral lesions, has removed this major obstacle. MRI, for example, has already allowed for the identification of discrete callosal fiber systems with their functional role specified (Gazzaniga et al., 1985; Gazzaniga, 1988a, 1988b). There remains, however, the problem of obtaining accurate maps of the human cortex, especially when one considers the incredible variation that exists in the patterning of the gyri and sulci, a pattern apparently as diverse as are fingerprints in the population.

It remains unclear to what extent a lesion in a given gyrus in one individual is functionally comparable to a similarly placed lesion in the same gyrus in another individual. The degree to which the functional fields are similarly distributed across individuals, the randomness with which secondary and tertiary sulcal folds position themselves during the growth of the cortex in late prenatal development, and the randomness with which various subzones of the functional fields are either entrapped within the sulcal walls or exposed on the gyral crests still remain to be determined. These questions might be approachable given techniques allowing us to look beyond the sulci to examine the full expanse of the cortical mantle.

Opportunities for Basic and Applied Research

The next generation of cortical maps should allow identification of landmarks both on the surface of the gyri and within the depths of the sulci, permitting measurement of the dimensions of cortical areas and lesions and clarifying the relations of damaged zones to surrounding cortical regions. Two kinds of cortical flat map techniques, straight line (SL) maps and contour (Ct) maps have emerged in the literature in the last several years. Until recently, these techniques have been applied only to studies of restricted cortical regions in nonhuman primates and cats. Each technique has as its goal the unfolding of the rounded, three-dimensional cerebral cortex into a map having the geometry of a table top, and each has its respective advantages and disadvantages.

The major goal of some new studies has been to demonstrate that straight-line two-dimensional (SL2D) flat maps can be constructed to represent extensive areas of the human cortex (Jouandet et al., 1987, in press). These studies chose not merely to open a restricted area of cortex, but undertook the most challenging test possible: the full unfolding of the entire human cerebral cortex. While MRI renders the human cortex immediately accessible, it remains very difficult to appreciate the dimension and relation of a cortical lesion vis-à-vis other cortical landmarks, when portions of the lesion and the landmarks are distributed over several individual brain slice images. SL2D maps take the next step in organizing the data. They open and unfold the cortex, simplify neocortical geometry, preserve the richness of its complexity, and fully represent the cortical territories in a manner providing the only adequate structural foundation on which functional information may, in the future, be interfaced in the construction of highly differentiated correlative maps. The promise of this new technique is that once users familiarize themselves with it, they will be able to see beyond the sulci and behold a landscape rich in previously obscured information and possibilities.

Bringing greater specificity to brain areas involved in cognition is the task of many enterprises, including the imaging techniques reviewed in the previous section. It is at this junction that the separate technologies begin to converge on common problems. Within the context of traditional neuropsychology, MRI combined with flat mapping of the cortical mantle will begin to provide the kind of greater specificity called for by modern cognitive theories.

The discussion in this section is not intended to convey the impression that all that is needed to understand human brain function are more detailed road maps of the human brain, particularly of the neocortex. The mapping techniques are discussed only as another technological accomplishment with implications for research on human brain processes and functions. It may well be the case that even the most up-to-date mapping will not provide a complete understanding of the dynamic patterns of activity in cortical neural processing. These ongoing patterns are the neurochemical bases for the observed plasticity of human behavior as manifested in development and change thoughout the life-span. Of particular interest is the transmission of nerve impulses and those processes associated with the ability of neurons to produce and release neurotransmitters (Iverson, 1979). Further research may address such questions as "Which neurotransmitters moderate or enhance which cognitive functions?" (See Lerner, 1984, for a theoretical discussion of these issues.)

4
Four New Technologies: Critical Problems

In this chapter we discuss some critical problems that must be resolved if the technologies are to contribute to the further development of cognitive science and its applications. Following some additional background on each technology, key problems with each technology are discussed. Among the six problems highlighted with respect to event-related brain potentials are definition and measurement issues, a lack of integration with the broader field of neuroscience, and undeveloped methodologies for field or clinical research. With regard to neuromagnetism, such problems as secondary sources, magnetically silent sources, and the inverse problem are discussed. Positron emission tomography presents such problems as the precise location of physiological processes, spatial and temporal discriminations, appropriate statistical analysis of the data, and risks to participants produced by the imaging technique. And studies of the effects of brain damage have been limited by problems of extrapolating from animal to human work. Moreover, in human studies, there has been a lack of understanding of the implications of effects of lesions for information processing.

EVENT-RELATED BRAIN POTENTIALS

Psychophysiology is a discipline that capitalizes on the fact that it is possible to measure the activity of bodily systems while people engage in a variety of cognitive and affect-producing tasks. The psychophysiologist's goal may be the understanding of the ways of the mind or the understanding of the ways of the brain. However, in both cases the psychophysiologist is building on the variation of the bodily systems measured and the circumstances of the measurement. The latter is the crucial point. Whether recording heart rate, evoked potentials, or metabolic activity in the brain, one is subject to the same basic constraint: the measurements are interpretable only within the context of the control that has been exercised over the subject's information-processing activities. One must guard against seduction by technological marvels, a seduction that often leads one to violate some of the basic tenets of psychophysiological research.

The precision and resolution with which the bodily systems are measured do not guarantee the quality of the study. One must devote an equal degree of care to the control of the experimental situation. Thus, if an investigator reports a relationship of "preparatory processes" to the amplitude of ERPs, or to the uptake of radioactive material by brain tissue, it is imperative that the preparatory processes be defined and measured with the same precision and care that is invested in the physiological measurements. The variation in the psychophysiological measurements (dependent variables) is of interest only if it can be related to the variations in task demands controlled by the experimenter (the independent variables). Often, neither type of variable is well defined in studies that search for relationships between them. Even if the dependent psychophysiological variables are measured with great precision, a careless definition of the independent task variables renders the experiment inadequate.

An investigator may, for example, employ a PET scan and publish results of examining the metabolism in different parts of the brain when people are asked to "think" compared with the metabolism when they are asked not to "think." The results appear exciting, especially as they are presented in color pictures that have anatomical reference. However, the results are largely uninterpretable because the putative independent variable, thinking versus nonthinking, is so poorly defined. There is so much that can differ between the two experimental conditions that it is quite inappropriate to claim that the study pertains to the relationship between thinking and metabolic rate. This error is not unique, of course, to PET studies. It has been committed by the practitioners of virtually all types of psychophysiology.

Problems arise, of course, in the definition and measurement of the dependent psychophysiological variables as well. We list here five of these difficulties, illustrated within the context of the study of event-related activities.

Definition of Components

The definition of the dependent variables presents a challenge to all psychophysiologists. In virtually every case the data are multidimensional and the measurement requires some method of selecting the features of the data to which the measurement will be applied. This is true whether the data take the form of two-dimensional maps or as multiple time series. There is, for example, a continuing controversy in the literature regarding the proper methods for defining an ERP component. The issue is clearly central. If two investigators purport to study the N200, it is imperative that they both, in fact, study the same component. That is, they must both use the same set of operations for extracting the amplitude of the N200 from their data. If one investigation uses the statistical technique known as principal component analysis and the other records the area under the curve in the interval between 150 and 250 msec after the stimulus, they may find themselves in conflict that is not justified by the data they were recording. There is at this time no consensual terminology and no systematic attempt to standardize measurement procedures to ensure that components are equivalently defined in all paradigms by all subjects (Fabiani et al., in press).

Overlapping Components

The problem of specified components is aggravated by the fact that the measures taken at any point in time reflect the activity of more than one process. For event response potentials and evoked response fields it is common to expect that the measures taken at any point in time represent the activity of more than one putative component. How to distinguish these components has been one of the more vexing problems in psychophysiology. Naatanen and Picton (1987), for example, suggested that at least five distinct components coexist in some form with the N100 in the same segment of the epoch. However, at the same time, their review demonstrates that despite the complexity it is possible, with the appropriate techniques, to study some of these components in isolation. The presence of multiple components complicates the interpretation of results. The challenge presented by this problem has motivated a number of investigators to focus attention on the refinement of both observational and statistical techniques.

Gaps in Neuroscience

We lack a full understanding of the generating sources of the various components of the ERP. It is also the case that we have insufficient understanding of the neurophysiological mechanisms underlying the phenomena observed in ERP research. It is generally agreed that we are observing the summed activity of synchronously activated neurons in ensembles whose fields are "open." But what is the actual role that these ensembles play (Allison, Wood, and McCarthy, 1986).

The most serious difficulty associated with this gap in our knowledge is that we are never quite sure how changes in the amplitude of the ERP should be interpreted. Donchin and Coles (in press) comment on this issue, in the context of a discussion of the P300. Their remarks, as quoted below, apply to other components as well:

> The first assumption is the weakest link in our entire structure. It is that the amplitude of the P300 is a measure of the extent to which the processor manifested by the P300 is activated, or "utilized."...It must be admitted, however, that we have no direct physiological evidence for this, or any other, interpretation of changes in the amplitude of the P300. It is plausible to assume that the larger the potential the larger the voltages generating the field which is being recorded and that this size is a measure of the activation of the tissue from which we record. This, unfortunately, is not necessarily the case as Allison et al. (1986) point out.
>
> ...For the time being, however, we must admit that the assumption is entertained primarily for its heuristic value and its merit must be evaluated according to its utility as a guide for future research. It should be noted, though, that the assumption does gain credence from the convergence of the very large number of studies conducted under its umbrella.

Difficulties With Clinical Studies

Making sense of the psychophysiological literature is a formidable task. The number of papers published annually is very large. Unfortunately, the literature contains many poor clinical papers, which are all too often case reports. While they serve an important function in the communication among clinicians, they are a poor source of data for developing theoretical structures. The methodological rigor of these studies is poor and the degree to which they are tied to the rest of the literature is inadequate. In part, this literature has been generated by the successful development of diagnostic tools based on psychophysiological methods. Instruments designed to serve well the needs of a clinician proliferate. These machines are often used in research projects even though they are not always designed with the needs of the researcher in mind. Thus, for example, many signal averagers, well designed for the diagnostic clinic, do not provide any means for saving the data associated with each trial in the test. They yield data only in the form of averages obtained over presentation of stimulus blocks. This is entirely adequate, even desirable, when conducting a diagnostic test, yet for many research projects it is critical to sort the data prior to averaging (e.g. to compare the ERP elicited when subjects erred or responded correctly, or to compare ERPs elicited when subjects were fast with those elicited when they were slow).

The Lack of a Normative Data Base

As this report shows, there is strong evidence supporting the assertion that psychophysiological measures can be used as tools in the study of cognitive function. However, this assertion is correct largely within the context of the laboratory. That is, the data serve well the needs of the theoretician who is trying to choose among models. It is the case that the variance among individuals observed in psychophysiological studies is sufficiently small to allow investigators to use small groups of subjects. As the research very often uses within-subject designs and is costly, investigators tend to use only 5-15 subjects in any study. One consequence is that there are very few normative data bases that indicate the expected pattern of recording in different nosological, age, and gender groups. This gap in knowledge is a serious impediment to the development of applications based on psychophysiological techniques. There is a serious need to conduct studies that would develop, for a carefully chosen set of experimental designs, a comprehensive normative data base that would allow the determination of the extent of variance in the measures that can be expected from various groups of individuals.

The technology of event-related brain potentials is quite similar to that of neuromagnetism. Similarity also exists with regard to fundamental problems that underly both methods. For example, the inverse problem discussed in the next section is also applicable to ERPs.

NEUROMAGNETISM: THE MAGNETOENCEPHALOGRAM

Magnetic fields accompany all moving electrical charges, including the ions that flow inside neurons. It is widely accepted that the neuromagnetic field normal to (perpendicular to) the scalp is due to intracellular current flow and is not affected significantly by extracellular volume currents. Although it is possible to detect the magnetic field associated with action potentials in isolated axons and nerve bundles (Swinney and Wikswo, 1980), the field observed outside the head is due largely to the flow of current in dendrites. Furthermore, the orientation of the path of the flowing current must be tangential to the surface of the skull if an external field radial to the scalp (emerging from or reentering the scalp) is to be detected. It is for this reason that the stronger sources of observed fields are believed to lie within sulci of the cortex. Neurons at gyri are predominantly normal in orientation relative to the scalp and would therefore contribute less to the observed external field.

The field associated with the flow of current in a single neuron would be too weak to be detected outside the scalp. In fact, it has been estimated that the simultaneous activity of about 10,000 neurons may result in a detectable field external to the scalp (Williamson and Kaufman, in press). Some field strengths are consistent with sources composed of 10,000 to 30,000 neurons. This is commensurate with the population of a cortical macrocolumn.

One motivation for studying neuromagnetic fields is that bone, cerebrospinal fluids, and other media are essentially transparent to low-frequency magnetic fields. These intervening tissues have radically different conductivities and therefore strongly affect the intracranial distribution of volume currents that underlie the EEG and the ERP. In analyzing neuromagnetic data it is therefore possible to ignore radial variations in conductivity within the head in computing the location, orientation, and strength of the underlying "source" of an observed field.

Six problems are discussed in this section.

Secondary Sources

Despite the claim of an intracellular origin for observed extracranial fields, it is theoretically possible for fields to arise from volume currents flowing at boundaries between two regions of different conductivity, thus giving rise to "secondary sources." These are likely to be associated with very weak fields and, if present, would be more likely to contaminate tangential fields rather than fields that are normal to the scalp. The effects on the radial field would be quite small. Nevertheless, it is important to precisely determine the magnitudes of contributions of secondary sources since, if they are significant but unaccounted for, they may bias computations of source locations and strengths.

Magnetically Silent Sources

As mentioned earlier, sources tangential to the surface of the skull are associated with observable fields, while so-called radial sources do not contribute to the external field. Assuming that these radial sources do not contribute significantly to the field external to the head, then many neurons in cortical gyri may be undetectable by magnetic sensors. In fact, Hari et al. (1982) found that the amplitude of the *electrical* N100 of the auditory evoked potential increases monotonically with interstimulus intervals (ISIs) up to 16 sec, while the amplitude of the *magnetic* N100 does not increase with ISI when it goes beyond 8 sec. This was taken as evidence that radial (magnetically silent) sources contribute to the electrical N100 and are responsible for the further increase in amplitude with ISI beyond 8 sec (see Naatanen and Picton, 1987). However, it should be noted that the magnetic responses were all recorded from over only one hemisphere, while the electrical responses were affected by sources in both hemispheres. Until it is demonstrated experimentally that the responses of the hemispheres are symmetrical at different ISIs, it is not proven that sources that are essentially silent magnetically can be detected electrically and that the behavior of these "silent" sources is significantly different from that of nonsilent magnetic sources. This is partly an empirical problem, and experiments are needed to cast further light onto it.

The problem we have just described may also be addressed in theoretical terms by simulating effects of different head shapes and source configurations on external fields predicted by physical law. Some efforts along these lines suggest that this problem may be of minor significance, but more work is needed.

Open Field and Closed Field Neurons

The classical distinction between open field and closed field neurons, made orginally by Lorente de No, applies to magnetic fields just as it does to electrical potentials measured at a distance. Theoretically, closed field neurons are silent both magnetically and electrically. This follows from the observation that their dendritic trees are symmetrical in three dimensions, and because of symmetry there is no net field to be observed at a distance. Open field neurons have a preferred average orientation, and this makes it possible for them to serve as sources for both magnetic fields and electrical potentials. It is desirable that we obtain some estimate of the proportions of neurons that may be characterized as closed field and the places in the brain where they are most numerous. It should be borne in mind, however, that approximate three-dimensional morphological symmetry does not suffice as a criterion for classifying a neuron as closed field. The pattern of current flowing in such neurons is the determining property, and we are not aware of data on how this pattern develops within dendritic trees of neurons of different types. However, it is worth noting that stellate cells predominate in visual cortex and, despite the high degree of three-dimensional symmetry exhibited by their dendritic trees, they probably make a major contribution to visual evoked responses. Therefore, the current paths within the dendrites of these cells must have preferred orientations. This observation leaves open the possibility that such cells located within gyri of the cortex may well contribute to external fields. This conjecture requires empirical evaluation.

Effects of Anatomical Symmetry

While the neurons of the visual cortex have a preferred orientation normal to its surface, stimulation of the entire central fovea will affect neurons on the medial surfaces of both hemispheres and in the roof and floor of the calcarine fissure as well. The roof and floor of the calcarine fissure have opposed orientations, as do the neurons of the two sides of the longitudinal fissure. These will exhibit opposed patterns of current flow, and their electrical and magnetic fields will tend to cancel each other, as do current flows in the dendrites of closed field neurons. Hence, both EP and EF experiments in which visual stimuli are presented to both hemi-retinas produce responses that represent the residual effect of the anatomical asymmetry of the hemispheres. It is possible to avoid this problem in vision by presenting critical stimuli to an octant or quadrant of visual field, but it is not obvious how to accomplish the same end when working in other modalities. Furthermore, this self-cancellation of fields and potentials due to populations of neurons having opposed orientations would affect both the spontaneous EEG and the MEG and needs to be carefully considered in their interpretation.

A Role for Complementary Technologies

The foregoing problems of concurrently active and opposed sources of populations of neurons cannot be resolved simply by improving the ways in which electrical and magnetic data are analyzed. While we must first discover how pervasive such problems are and where they are most likely to arise, there is a compelling need for the use of complementary technologies. Since the use of complementary methods is not widespread, the failure to employ them constitutes an important problem for advancing the study of cognitive psychophysiology. For example, high resolution and accurately scaled MRI scans together with reviews of histological data on all areas of the human brain may furnish computational theorists with information useful in estimating the proportion of closed field neurons in the brain and of areas in which there is significant mirror symmetry. Furthermore, PET technology applied in experiments in which human subjects are exposed to precisely the same conditions as are subjects used in studies of spontaneous, evoked, and event-related electrical and magnetic activity could provide a great deal of evidence as to whether significant areas of the brain are "invisible" to these methods. By the same token, evidence of electrical or magnetic activity from a region showing little metabolic activity would undoubtedly be of considerable interest.

The Inverse Problem

Many of the foregoing problems are related to the general statement that there is no unique solution to what is called the inverse problem. Given a known source or array of sources within a conducting volume whose properties are known, it is possible to determine the field or potential that would be detected outside the volume. This forward problem does have a unique solution; however, the converse is not true. Given complete knowledge of the external field or the distribution of potentials, it is still not possible to arrive at a unique solution in which a particular source is known to account for the observed phenomena. A large number of sources could produce the same external field. Therefore, there is a need to constrain inverse solutions by use of knowledge from other domains of science and, as stated above, also by use of complementary technologies. For example, considerable knowledge already exists of the organization of the primary projection areas in humans, and it is known that the somatosensory homunculus represents the order of representation of different portions of the body along the posterior bank of the central sulcus. Straightforward measurements of the somatosensory evoked field produce data in excellent agreement with this physiologically established ordering, thus providing face validity for the inverse solutions that have been presented.

Similarly, MRI scans of human subjects who had served in evoked fields experiments can show that the computed source locations lie at positions in various sulci known to contain neurons that respond to the particular sensory stimuli. Moving a visual stimulus into the peripheral retina results in a corresponding migration of the computed current dipole source into the depth of the longitudinal sulcus, and the magnitude of this variation with eccentricity is in approximate agreement with the known cortical magnification factor. To be sure, ambiguity increases when studying less well-known portions of the brain, and it is difficult to decide among alternative inverse solutions. This problem can also be ameliorated by conjoint use of PET technology.

It should be noted that many portions of the brain react in serial rather than parallel fashion to a particular sensory input. Thus, for example, N100 and P200 of the auditory evoked fields occur at different times, and their sources have been shown to be separated by a distance of about 1 cm. If both of these portions were to be active at the same time, then it might prove difficult, although not impossible, to resolve them. However, the time differences also serve to ameliorate the problem of source resolution.

A Final Note on Neuromagnetism

The technical problems discussed in this section are critical. Until further progress is made toward resolving them, it is unlikely that significant progress will be made in applications of the technology to the study of cognitive processes, except perhaps in very fundamental programs as discussed in Chapter 3 in the section on research findings. The use of complementary technologies appears promising: certain problems characteristic of particular technologies can indeed be offset by using several approaches in a particular study or research program. However, it is also necessary to address the technical and physiological problems in the context of conceptual questions posed by cognitive science. Those questions serve to reinforce the connection between cognitive and physiological processes. They should influence decisions about the way in which neuromagnetism and other technologies are developed and used in experimental work.

IMAGING TECHNIQUES I: POSITRON EMISSION TOMOGRAPHY

Positron emission tomography is a complex technology requiring adequate human and physical resources in the areas of instrumentation, radiochemistry, tracer kinetics, computer programming, and neurobiology as well as easy access to patients and normal control subjects. Truly successful programs have managed to gather together into one group individuals with expertise in all of these areas, usually in the setting of a large university teaching hospital. The major physical resources necessary to complement such a team of investigators include a medical cyclotron, a PET scanner, a large minicomputer, and radiochemistry laboratories. At the present time there are approximately 20 PET centers in academic medical institutions in the United States. Less than half of these centers have yet to assemble the necessary staffing required to do good neurobiological research with PET. The reason for this is twofold: (1) lack of trained personnel and (2) a failure to realize the importance of this need.

In addition to the more general needs of PET in terms of staffing, equipment, and patients, there are also several areas of concern with regard to the actual performance of PET studies. These include the anatomical localization of regions of interest within a PET scan, the spatial resolution of PET, the temporal resolution of PET, and the statistical analysis of PET data. We deal briefly with each of these issues.

Anatomical Localization

Determining the relationship between physiology and anatomy is one of the objectives of most functional studies with PET, including all of those designed to understand cognitive processes. Although physiological images of the brain often contain some anatomical information, correspondence between physiology and anatomy cannot be assumed. Despite this fact, some investigators have based their judgments about anatomical localization on the appearance of the physiological PET image of blood flow or glucose uptake. This practice is not satisfactory.

An anatomical localization procedure for physiological imaging has been developed and validated (Fox, Perlmutter, and Raichle, 1985). This approach determines the anatomical location of a PET region of interest with the coordinate system of atlases for stereotaxic neurological surgery. Measurements made from a lateral skull radiograph and from a tomographic transmission scan form the basis of this method. The method is accurate and objective and does not depend on visual inspection of the image. Regions defined by this procedure can be easily compared among subjects in a study and among different subject populations within a laboratory. Comparisons of data from different laboratories are also possible when this procedure is employed. Acceptance of such a method by people using PET is essential.

Spatial Resolution

Spatial resolution has always been a concern to investigators contemplating the use of PET for physiological studies. Operationally, the spatial resolution of PET is based on the spatial distribution of measured radioactivity produced by a single point source of radioactivity. This spatial distribution of radioactivity is a blurred representation of the original point source with the highest counting rate at its center. The resolution of a PET system is defined as the width of this distribution of radioactivity at one half of the maximum counting rate, the so-called full width at half maximum, usually abbreviated FWHM. One very important consequence of this definition of resolution is that when two point sources of radioactivity occur simultaneously in the field of view of a PET device, they cannot be distinguished as two separate sources if they are closer than a distance of one FWHM. Furthermore, accurate quantification of radioactivity in a particular region of the brain requires that the region be approximately twice the FWHM in all dimensions. PET devices currently operational have spatial resolutions, defined as the FWHM, in the range of 10-15 mm. The ultimate resolution of PET defined in this way has not been clearly established but will be limited by factors such as the distance traveled in tissue by the positron before annihilation, usually about 2-3 mm; slight deviation of the paths of the two annihilation photons from colinearity; and the statistical quality of the data. It is realistic to anticipate that reconstruction for some PET images to a resolution of 5-6 mm will be possible, although this is still less than optimal for some work.

Functional studies with PET, including those of importance to cognitive psychophysiology, allow an additional, very important perspective on the issue of spatial resolution. By functional studies is meant studies in which some type of activation paradigm is employed to produce a change in local blood flow or metabolism from a resting or control state. Under such circumstances PET data, obtained from the subtractions of a control state image from an image obtained during some type of functional activity, can be used to determine whether areas separated by significantly less than one FWHM are differentially activated by specific alterations in stimulus conditions (Fox et al., 1985). This expectation is based on signal detection theory, which has also been used to explain an equivalent phenomenon in visual processing known as hyperacuity. The occurrence of a source of radioactivity against a background or control state can be localized using special computer-based algorithms as a shift in the point of maximum change in radioactivity from the control state (Fox et al., 1985). Current PET devices permit response localization with an accuracy of 1-2 mm using instruments with an inherent resolution of 18 mm (Fox et al., 1985). Experimental strategy defines the operational resolution of such a study. The ability of PET to spatially discriminate sequential changes in local radioactivity in this manner has important implications for the study of very discrete functional activity in the human brain, provided that experimental protocols are designed to take advantage of it. Anticipated improvements in the inherent spatial resolution of future PET scanners, possibly as good as 3-5 mm FWHM, are likely to make future spatial discriminations of this type quite refined (e.g., 300-400 microns).

Temporal Resolution

The temporal resolution of studies with PET vary greatly depending on the choice of tracer strategy. For example, measurements of metabolism require 45 minutes, whereas measurements of blood flow can be made in less than 1 minute. Temporal resolution also varies with the choice of radioisotope (i.e., for ^{18}F the half-life is 110 minutes, whereas for ^{15}O, the half-life is 2 minutes). The measurement of local brain glucose consumption using ^{18}F-fluorodeoxyglucose (Phelps et al., 1979; Reivich et al., 1979) requires 45 minutes to accomplish once the tracer has been prepared and administered. The resulting measurement of local glucose utilization is a summary of events during this entire period of time weighted according to the shape of the arterial concentration of the tracer. A feature of any study of functional activation is the need for second measurements on the same individual (e.g., Peterson et al., 1988). Thus if a control state PET image is subtracted from a stimulated state image to localize areas of activation, then the time necessary to make the measurement as well as for radioactivity to clear from the body becomes very important. The time necessary for radioactivity to clear is governed by the physical, as well as the biological, half-life of the tracer. In the case of ^{18}F this time is about nine hours. Times of this magnitude obviously make difficult a second study in the same individual on the same day. As a result, most functional studies of the human brain with PET and fluorodeoxyglucose involve a single measurement in each subject studied with control measurements from a separate group of subjects. When a single subject has been studied more than once with fluorodeoxyglucose and PET, the measurements have usually not been made on the same day.

Because of the exquisite sensitivity of blood flow to local changes in neuronal activity plus the speed (40 seconds—Raichle et al., 1983) and ease with which it can be measured and repeated in a single subject (up to 10 measurements in a single sitting), it would appear to be the ideal method for functional mapping with PET.

Statistical Analysis

The statistical analysis of PET data is an especially challenging problem. The average PET measurement provides 7 or more slices of the human brain. Within such a data set it is possible to identify a very large number of regions of interest. However, in so doing, one runs into the very difficult problem of multiple comparisons leading to the false identification of regions significantly different from the control. In much of the early PET work this problem was often ignored. Simple paired and unpaired t-tests were used to evaluate large data sets. In retrospect, it is very difficult to know the true significance of much of these data, suggesting that caution be taken in making interpretations. Recently, more sophisticated approaches to the statistical analysis of such data have been developed (see Petersen et al., 1988), which now provide an opportunity to use all the available data.

Risks to Participants

The risk to participants in PET imaging studies is small but present due to exposure to the effects of ionizing radiation. The U.S. Food and Drug Administration (FDA) has established strict guidelines for the exposure of normal subjects to ionizing radiation in the course of research. These guidelines reflect limits established as safe for workers over age 18 exposed to radiation during the course of their employment. Subjects under age 18 are allowed to receive only 10 percent of this dose. These limits are strictly enforced by the FDA through local radioactive drug research committees or investigational new drug applications. It is always viewed as a necessary goal of all studies involving PET not only to keep radiation exposure below the FDA limits but also to keep exposure to the lowest possible amount consistent with obtaining adequate data. Gains can be anticipated in reducing radiation by improving the efficiency of PET imaging devices dedicated to functional brain imaging in normal human subjects. This task already is under way: because of the importance of PET to functional imaging of the human brain, there is a great deal of support for research on ways to reduce radiation exposure to normal subjects undergoing PET scanning. This includes instrumentation developments as well as improved software for image reconstruction.

IMAGING TECHNIQUES II: MAGNETIC RESONANCE IMAGING

While in vivo MRI provides highly specific information, it suffers from a lack of sensitivity. The strength of the signal produced by a particular nucleus is the product of its magnetic moment, its abundance in nature, and its concentration in the tissue. McGeer (1983) calculated this product or "imaging index" for a number of nuclei and compared them with hydrogen. The results indicate that the detectable signal from ^{31}P or ^{23}Na, the next most promising nuclei in terms of signal strength, is reduced by a factor of more than 10,000, while the potential signal from ^{13}C is more than five orders of magnitude less than hydrogen. Reductions in signal intensity of these magnitudes prohibit the reconstruction of images with the spatial resolution exhibited for protons. Thus, MRI must be limited to very low resolution studies for nuclei other than protons.

COGNITIVE STUDIES IN BRAIN ALTERATIONS OR DAMAGE

Research on both animals and humans with brain lesions has made important contributions to the understanding of the kinds of information processed by large zones of brain tissue. This is particularly true when considering sensory systems such as vision, audition, touch, and olfaction. Recent work on primates has also illuminated more complex processes such as how the brain manages attention (Wurtz et al., 1980). In humans, the brain-damaged patient has also revealed which hemisphere is involved in language and speech and which lobes are involved in memory, thought, sequencing behaviors, emotions, and other mental phenomena (Nass and Gazzaniga, 1987).

The challenge to this approach comes from the greater sophistication of current theories about the composition of a particular mental activity. As cognitive theories become more precise, there is a greater interest in identifying more specific brain correlates. A lesion that produces a disorder in language processing must now be categorized in precise cognitive terms. More pointedly, smaller and more defined brain lesions are sought that may disrupt language in a limited and discrete manner in an effort to confirm current theories about the modular organization of language function (Swinney et al., 1989). It is still the belief of many students of linguistics that discrete brain lesions may disrupt particular grammatical rules or at least disrupt lexical modules versus phrasal modules.

Furthermore, seeing how other processes such as attention or spatial mechanisms contribute to language processing is currently of interest. Here, too, the large lesion approach seriously limits progress in this area (Posner et al., 1988).

Another very important problem is how work on animals and work on humans relate to one another. Does a lesion in the hippocampus create the same problems for the rat or the monkey as it does for the human? Some investigators feel there are analogous findings with similar lesions to such structures (Squire, 1987), although others disagree (Lynch and Baudry, 1988). We now know that structures like the superior colliculus contribute different functions in the monkey (Wurtz and Albano, 1980) than in humans (see Holtzman, 1984). The same is true for lesions to the anterior commissure (Gazzaniga, 1987). Such differences argue for caution in attempts to extrapolate results obtained from animals to humans. It is even more difficult to develop implications from the animal work for linguistic and other higher-order processes.

CRITICAL PROBLEMS

Finally, there are serious problems concerning how to interpret the behavioral changes subsequent to a brain lesion with regard to the role of the brain areas affected in cognitive processing modules. At the cellular level, it is now known that altering inputs to a cell can radically change the postsynaptic receptors of a cell and thereby alter its response characteristics. At the level of systems, how can a lesion that produces damage in site A tell you about site A anymore than it tells you about the network that site A is a part of? Site A can be connected to dozens of other centers as well as receiving inputs from dozens of other sites. Loss of tonic or inhibitory influences in a neural network can have possible profound effects on the kinds of information a system can process. Although this problem is generally recognized, it is also generally repressed. Yet, as Francis Crick has said, the lesion approach, whether one likes it or not, is one of the few approaches available to the brain scientist.

5
Applications and Ethical Considerations

Attempts to use the technologies described in this report as well as others for applied purposes raise a number of ethical issues. Most prominent in the public media are concerns about another technology, the use of lie detectors, which is also based on the assessment of physiological processes. Questions include how accurate these devices are and whether they should be used for making administrative decisions. Although the technologies discussed in this report have not received a comparable amount of public attention, their use raises the same issues of accuracy and ethics. With regard to accuracy, in this chapter we discuss the nature of the data, the "language of the brain," and psychological meaning. With regard to ethics, we discuss the issues of invasion of privacy and the dangers of commercialization.

Of primary interest to the Army are potential applications of the technologies for purposes of selection and training. We know of no attempts to date to use any of the techniques discussed in this report for these purposes. Although it is true that considerable progress has been made in laboratory and field research, there are still a number of problems to be resolved, as discussed earlier. Moreover, the necessary development and implementation work has not been done. Until the problems are resolved and progress is made in development, it would be premature to use these technologies for operational purposes. Nevertheless, the fact that the technologies are in the public domain and have been used in clinical contexts makes it tempting to consider adopting them for use in other applied settings. And the temptation increases as rapid advances in engineering place new, more advanced tools in the marketplace, further facilitating their use as quick fixes to difficult problems. We address these issues below.

ISSUES PRESENTED BY THE DATA

Consider the issues raised by the data on such ERP components as the P300. There are any number of applications for such a procedure. However, if one is offered a box in which a pointer is driven to the right or to the left by the magnitude of the P300, which varies, in turn, as a function of some mental process, two classes of questions arise.

First, there is the question of utility. Does the technique really work? To date there has not been an ecologically valid test of the P300-based procedures, with the exception of some of the more clinical applications. We know the procedures work well in complex laboratory arrangements, yet there has never been support for thorough experimentation in normative situations. This issue is, to a large extent, open.

Second, there is the issue of privacy. What is the degree to which monitoring impinges on individual rights? Does it go beyond currently accepted interpretation of the rules? There is a popular notion that it will be possible to achieve the technical feat of making audible by mechanical means those thoughts that constitute our internal speech. The metaphor driving the worry is that of eavesdropping.

Eavesdropping on the mind is unlikely. It would only be possible if the signals we can record externally carry within them the richness and the variety available in mental life. One can fantasize, of course, that new technologies will increase the range of the monitoring. Indeed, given the trends in increased computing power and reduced size and cost, super minicomputers implemented on biological principles might have the power and the savvy to interpret the signals to a depth that matches the profundity of the task. However, even in that case psychophysiological eavesdropping would not be possible.

To some extent, the constraints that could not be eliminated stem from the fact that there is too much noise to develop a useful eavesdropping technique. There are far too many processes all working in parallel and furiously interacting with each other for there to be a possibility that an external manifestation of any of these processes will "talk" to a computer in the same language it "talks" to its counterparts in the system.

The matter of the language of the brain is crucial here. The implementation of thought processes is ultimately a matter of neurons communicating with other neurons. Indeed, it is most likely a matter of millions of neurons talking to millions of other neurons for any thought to occur. These neurons converse with each other, of course, by whatever language is used for such communication. There is no consensus as to the nature of the language. It is clear that neurons affect other neurons by secreting tiny doses of chemicals (the neurotransmitters). These secretions are the consequence of the conduction of neuronal impulses across synapses and the integrative activities of the dendritic membranes.

Cognitive psychophysiologists benefit from the fact that, when occurring in the mass and in a highly synchronous manner, these interneuronal transactions manifest themselves on the scalp in the form of large integrated fields of potentials recorded as the EEG. If labeled radioactively, they may manifest themselves to an imaging device. However, this activity, while valuable as an index for the time course and level of neuronal action, is unlikely to serve as a source of information on the specific nature of the vast exchanges in the neuron's own language that have given rise to these psychophysiological signals.

MONITORING PARADIGMS AND CONSTRAINTS

One can assume that psychophysiological signals will be useful only if what is being monitored is defined scientifically. We do not, and will not, eavesdrop on the mind. Rather, we are observing the consequences of neural action and, by judicious construction of the situation, we may be able to pose questions that the psychophysiological signals may answer. Describing psychophysiological monitoring as a process of seeking answers to specific questions is very important because it underlines the principal condition for the success of such monitoring. The value of the answer will depend on the sagacity with which the question has been put. In other words, the key to the usefulness of these approaches is the ability to pose useful questions rather than the procurement of yet another measuring instrument.

Proper application of psychophysiological monitoring requires that one realize that what is being monitored is the activity of bodily systems. These systems are driven for physiological reasons by the demands on the system. These bodily organs serve more than one function and therefore their activity cannot be presumed to be uniquely related to any psychological construct.

The signals we record make sense, therefore, only in terms of the situation. There is no deception wave—a wave that no matter when and under what circumstances it has been recorded indicates that a person has lied. There is not even a wave that indicates unequivocally that *any* emotion has occurred. Rather, the change in the physical signal indicates the activation of a certain processor or processors. If, and only if, this is uniquely interpretable within the context of the recording is it possible to make psychological inferences from the data.

Thus, the degree to which psychophysiological signals can have psychological meaning depends on the degree to which the system is set to be driven in a unique fashion by the psychological variables. For example, the workload assessment techniques employing the P300 depend on the establishment of a very sensitive relationship between the conditions of measurement and the subject's understanding of the situational demands. In other words, active participation of the subject is a condition for the success of psychophysiological monitoring. It is unlikely that it would be possible to apply a probe that will intrude on the subject without, at some level, the subject's accepting the structuring of the situation that constitutes the question addressed to the system.

The above remarks should not be construed as casting doubt on the usefulness of psychophysiological monitoring. The increasing depth to which these signals are understood and the increasing sophistication of cognitive models when coupled with the spectacular developments in miniaturization, sensor technology, and data analysis open a very broad scope for such monitoring. However, this will be accomplished only within the constraints of good methodology. Furthermore, whatever monitoring can be done will be constrained by the nature of the biological and psychological systems involved. One must steer clear of extravagant claims and avoid the unnecessary fears that these might invoke.

DANGERS OF COMMERCIALIZATION

It must be emphasized that the remarks made in the previous section pertain to the scientifically valid use of the techniques. We must also point out that the limits that science and nature impose on feasibility do not always serve as constraints on the selling of technological marvels. Reason and proper scientific analysis suggest that eavesdropping on the mind is unlikely. Unfortunately, this does not imply that someone with a gadget and a good marketing technology cannot attempt to persuade the public, as individuals and through their government, that some technical marvel has been achieved.

From snake oil to water divining to more contemporary panaceas, those who peddle worthless solutions to serious problems have often been able to induce belief in the efficacy of some technique despite the caveats of science.

CONCLUSION

This chapter has addressed the issue of the scientific feasibility and validity of monitoring individuals by certain psychophysiological techniques. The conclusions reached should contribute to a more cautious approach taken by policy makers in government and industry. There is of course no guarantee that these cautions will in fact be heeded. Policy makers are often under pressure to adopt techniques that address specific problems that are not easily resolved. They may be tempted by the availability of a variety of easy-to-use techniques that purport to deal with those problems. Under such circumstances, it is conceivable that vast systems for monitoring individuals could be implemented. The fact that they are without scientific value will not reduce their potential social impact.

6
Expanding the Domain

The necessary conceptual foundations are in place for a hybrid psychophysiological-cognitive science approach to the study of brain functions and behavior. The prospect exists of significant progress if researchers can be motivated to adopt this approach. We have argued in this report that a combination of these fields is likely to yield significant benefits. Three broad areas, in particular, would be enhanced:

- Psychological testing. To the extent that we can discover the functional units underlying cognitive processing, it will become possible to measure their effectiveness. Having done so, we should be able to better understand the way people perform specific types of tasks.
- Computer systems. The best argument for the possibility that a computer system can behave intelligently is the existence of another such mechanism. It is thus not surprising that many researchers in artificial intelligence model their computer systems on what is known about cognitive function in humans. An enhanced understanding of the functional organization of the brain into distinct processing components may have a direct impact on ways in which computer systems are constructed, making these systems more sophisticated.
- Medical diagnoses. Better characterization of brain function will allow one to specify more accurately the nature of a deficit following brain damage. Conversely, one will also be able to specify more accurately the nature of the intact functions, after brain damage, information that will be valuable for rehabilitation.

It is also the case, however, that several issues must be addressed if the new approach is to be adequately implemented. These issues fall into three categories: domains, resources, and education. Each of these issues would be on the agenda of an expanded study to consider the state of the art in terms of possible research breakthroughs and feasible applications.

DOMAINS

As areas most likely to benefit quickly from cognitive psychophysiology, vision, attention, and memory are good candidates because much is known about them, cognitively, computationally, and psychophysiologically. In order to explore the extent to which the approach can be extended at the present time to other domains, experts in various specialized areas of psychophysiology, in computational theorizing, in computer software and hardware, and in cognitive psychology should be involved. It is particulary important to involve experts in such fields as artificial intelligence, fuzzy logic and sets, computer simulation of neural networks, biological integrated circuits, and biophysics.

Questions include whether psychophysiological techniques can be readily applied, whether appropriate cognitive methodologies are available, and whether computational theorizing and computer science more generally have progressed to the point at which useful hypotheses can be formulated.

RESOURCE LIMITATIONS

Given the problems with drawing inferences from brain-damaged patients noted in Chapter 4, the preferred psychophysiological data are measures of brain activation in normal subjects while they perform a task. However, there simply are not enough available facilities to enable cognitive scientists to exploit these techniques. The main problem is that scientists need time to explore and improvise, to learn while doing; good experiments evolved from preliminary explorations of pilot work. At present, the available neuroimaging facilities are oversubscribed, and such opportunities are not available. An enlarged committee could be charged with devising ways to use available resources most effectively and to expand such resources.

EDUCATION

Even if sufficient facilities were available, most cognitive scientists would not know how to use them, nor would many necessarily be interested in doing so. Similarly, psychophysiologists typically are not motivated to learn the necessary technical information and skills to engage in computational theorizing. In all likelihood, the different segments of the community will be motivated to expand their approaches only when three conditions are met: (1) There must be few demonstrations of the usefulness of such hybrid approaches. Initial examples are just now being provided, and this condition will probably be satisfied in the near future. (2) There must be a relatively easy way for researchers to acquire a working knowledge of the necessary information and skills. Something along the lines of the McDonnell Summer Institute in Cognitive Neuroscience may be appropriate. (3) There must be adequate funding for such work. An expanded study should include consideration of each of these concerns.

CONCLUSION

The issues discussed in this chapter could form the basis for an enlarged study of the relationship between neuroscience and cognitive science. The study would be broadly interdisciplinary and should be conducted by experts in the various specialized areas. It would focus on both the conceptual issues that must be resolved for further progress and on the kinds of scientific breakthroughs needed for application of the technologies. The study would also address the institutional changes that may be required for facilitating interdisciplinary research. Two proposed innovations discussed in this chapter are increased access to appropriate facilities for research and the establishment of programs to prepare and encourage investigators to engage in the kind of collaborative work needed for development of the field.

References

Allison, T., C.C. Wood, and G. McCarthy
    1986   The central nervous system. Pg. 5-25 in M.G.H. Coles, E. Donchin, and S.W. Porges (Eds.), *Psychophysiology: Systems, Processes, and Applications*. New York: Guilford Press.

Anderson, J.R.
    1978   Arguments concerning representations for mental imagery. *Psychological Review* 85:249-277.
    1983   Spreading activation. Pp. 61-90 in J.R. Anderson and S.M. Kosslyn (Eds.), *Tutorials in Learning and Memory: Essays in Honor of Gordon H. Bower*. San Francisco: W.H. Freeman.

Arthur, D.L., and A. Starr
    1984   Task-relevant late positive component of the auditory event-related potential in monkey resembles P300 in humans. *Science* 223:186-188.

Barth, D., J. Beatty, J. Broffman, and W. Sutherling
    1986   Magnetic localization of a current dipole source implanted in a sphere and a human cadaver. *EEG Clin. Neurophysiol.* 63:260-273.

Barth, D., J. Sutherling, J. Engle, Jr., and J. Beatty
    1984   Neuromagnetic evidence for spatially distributed sources underlying epileptiform spikes in the human brain. *Science* 223:293-296.

Begleiter, H.P., B. Porjesz, and B. Kissin
    1984   Event-related potentials in boys at risk for alcoholism. *Science* 225:1493-1496.

Brenner, D., S.J. Williamson, and L. Kaufman
    1975   Visually evoked magnetic fields of the human brain. *Science* 190:480-482.

Broca, P.
    1981   Remarques sur le siege de la faculte du langage articule. *Bulletin of Social Anatomy of Paris* 36:330-357.

Brooks, D.J., A.A. Lammertsma, B.P. Beaney, K.L Leenders, P.D. Buckingham, J. Marchall, and T. Jones
    1984   Measurement of regional cerebral pH in human subjects using continuous inhalation of $^{11}CO_2$ and positron emission tomography. *Journal of Cerebral Blood Flow & Metabolism* 4:458-465.

Buchwald, J., and L. Dickerson
    1987   Effects of associate cortex ablation on cat mid-latency evoked potentials. *Neuroscience Abstracts* 13:1267.

Callaway, E., P. Tueting, and S. Koslow (Eds.)
    1978   *Brain Event-Related Potentials in Man.* New York: Academic Press.

Chapman, R.M., G.L. Romani, S. Barbanera, R. Leoni, I. Modena, G.B. Ricci, and F. Campitelli
    1983   SQUID instrumentation and the relative covariance method for magnetic 3-D localization of pathological cerebral sources. *Lett. al Nuovo Cimento* 38:549-554.

Coles, M.G.H., E. Donchin, and S.W. Porges
    1986   *Psychophysiology: Systems, Processes and Applications.* New York: Guilford Press.

Coles, M.G.H., G. Gratton, T.R. Bashore, C.W. Eriksen, and E. Donchin
    1985   A psychophysiological investigation of the continuous flow model of human information processing. *Journal of Experimental Psychology: Human Perception and Performance* 11:529-553.

Coles, M.G.H., G. Gratton, A.F. Kramer, and G.A. Miller
    1986   Principles of signal acquisition and analysis. In M.G.H. Coles, E. Donchin, and S.W. Porges (Eds.), *Psychophysiology: Systems, Processes and Applications.* New York: Guilford Press.

Curtis, S., L. Kaufman, and S.J. Williamson
    1988   Divided attention revisited: Selection based on location or pitch. In K. Atsumi, T. Katila, M. Kotani, S.J. Williamson, and S. Ueno (Eds.), *Biomagnetism '87, Proceedings of the 6th International Conference on Biomagnetism.* Tokyo: Denki University Press.

Cushing, H.
    1932   *Intracranial Tumors: Notes Upon Two Thousand Verified Cases.* Springfield: Thames.

Deadwyler, S.A., M.O. West, E.P. Christian, R.E. Hampson, and T.C. Foster
    1985   Sequence-related changes in sensory-evoked potentials in the dentate gyrus: A mechanism for item-specific short-term information storage in the hippocampus. *Behavioral and Brain Sciences.*

Deutsch, J.A., and D. Deutsch
    1963   Attention: Some theoretical considerations. *Psychology Review* 70:80-90.

Donchin, E.
    1981   Surprise? ... Surprise! *Psychophysiology* 18:493-513.

Donchin, E., and M.G.H. Coles
    in press   Is the P300 component a manifestation of context updating? *Behavioral and Brain Sciences.*

REFERENCES

Donchin, E., D. Karis, T. Bashore, M. Coles, and G. Gratton
    1986   Cognitive psychophysiology and human information processing. In M.G.H. Coles, E. Donchin, and S. Porges (Eds.), *Psychophysiology: Systems, Processes, and Applications*. New York: Guilford Press.

Druckman, D., D. Karis, and E. Donchin
    1983   Information-processing in bargaining: Reactions to an opponent's shift in concession strategy. In R. Tietz (Ed.), *Aspiration Levels in Bargaining and Economic Decision Making*. Berlin-Heidelberg-New York: Springer.

Dusser de Barrene, I.G.
    1916   Experimental researches on sensory localizations in the cerebral cortex. *Quarterly Journal of Experimental Physiology* 9:355-390.

Fabiani, M., G. Gratton, D. Karis, and E. Donchin
    in press   The definition, identification, and reliability of measurement of the P300 component of the event-related brain potential. In P.K. Ackles, J.R. Jennings, and M.G.H. Coles (Eds.), *Advances in Psychophysiology*, Vol. 2. Greenwich, Conn.: JAI Press, Inc.

Fischler, I., P.A. Bloom, D.G. Childers, S.E. Roucos, and N.W. Perry, Jr.
    1983   Brain potentials related to stages of sentence verification. *Psychophysiology* 20:400-409.

Fischler, I., D.G. Childers, T. Achaiyapaopan, and N.W. Perry
    1985   Brain potential during sentence verification: Automatic aspects of comprehension. *Biological Psychology* 21:83-105.

Fischler, I., Y-S Jin, T.L. Boaz, N.W. Boaz, and D.G. Childers
    1987   Brain potentials related to seeing one's own name. *Brain and Language* 30:245-262.

Fox, P.T., J.S. Perlmutter, and M.E. Raichle
    1985   A stereotactic method of anatomical localization for positron emission tomography. *Journal of Computer Assisted Tomography* 9:141-153.

Freeman, W.J.
    1975   *Mass Action in the Nervous System*. New York: Academic Press.

Fritsch, G., and E. Hitzig
    1870   Uber die electrishe Erregbarkeit des Grosshirne. *Arch. Anat. Physiol.* 37:300-332.

Garnett, E.S., G. Firnau, and C. Nahmias
    1983   Dopamine visualized in the basal ganglia of living man. *Nature* 305:137-138.

Gazzaniga, M.S.
    1985   *The Social Brain*. New York: Basic Books.
    1987   Cognitive and neurologic aspects of hemispheric disconnection in the human brain. Discussions in *Neuroscience* FESN Vol. IV, No. 4.
    1988a   *Perspectives in Memory Research*. Cambridge, Mass.: MIT Press.
    1988b   *Mind Matters*. Boston: Houghton Mifflin.

Gazzaniga, M.S., and R.W. Sperry
    1967   Language after section of the cerebral commissures. *Brain* 90:131-148.

Gazzaniga, M.S., J.D. Holtzman, M.D.F. Deck, and B.C.P. Lee
 1985   MRI assessment of human callosal surgery with neuropsychological correlates. *Neurology* 35:1763-1766.
Goodin, D.S., K. Squires, and A. Starr
 1978   Long latency event-related components of the auditory evoked potential in dementia. *Brain* 101:635-648.
Gopher, D., and E. Donchin
 1986   Workload—An examination of the concept. In K.R. Boff, L. Kaufman, and J.P. Thomas (Eds.), *Handbook of Perception and Human Performance, Vol II. Cognitive Processes and Performance.* New York: Wiley & Sons.
Gudden, B.
 1870   Experimentaluntersuchungen uber das periphere und central nerven system. *Arch. Psychiat. Nerven* 693-723.
Hari, R., K. Kaila, T. Katila, T. Tuomisto, and T. Varpulo
 1982   Interstimulus interval dependence of the auditory vertex response and its magnetic counterpart: Implications for their neural generation. *EEG and Clinical Neurophysiology* 54:461-569.
Hari, R., K. Reinikainen, E. Kaukaranta, M. Mamalainen, R. Ilmoniemi, A. Penttinen, J. Salamen, and D. Teszner
 1984   Somatosensory evoked cerebral magnetic fields from SI and SII in man. *EEG and Clin. Neurophysiol.* 58: 467-473.
Hayes-Roth, F.
 1979   Distinguishing theories of representation: A critique of Anderson's "Arguments concerning mental imagery." *Psychological Review* 86:376-392.
Herscovitch, P., M.E. Raichle, M.R. Kolbourn, and M.J. Welch
 1987   Positron emission tomographic measurement of cerebral blood flow and permeability-surface area product of water using ^{15}O-water and ^{11}C-butanol. *Journal of Cerebral Blood Flow and Metabolism* 7:527-542.
Hillyard, S.A., and T.E. Picton
 1987   Electrophysiology of cognition. In F. Plum (Ed.), *Handbook of Physiology.* Baltimore: William and Wilkins.
Hillyard, S.A., and J.C. Hansen
 1986   Attention: Electrophysiological approaches. Pp. 227-243 in M.G.H. Coles, E. Donchin and S. Proges (Eds.), *Psychophysiology: Systems, Processes, and Applications.* New York: Guilford Press.
Hillyard, S.A., and M. Kutas
 1983   Electrophysiology of cognitive processing. Pp. 33-61 in M.R. Rosenzweig and L.W. Porter (Eds.), *Annual Review of Psychology,* Vol. 34. Palo Alto, Calif.: Annual Reviews, Inc.
Hillyard, S.A., R.F. Hink, V.L. Schwent, and T.W. Picton
 1973   Electrical signs of selective attention in the human brain. *Science* 182:177-180.
Hochberg, J.E.
 1968   Attention, organization and consciousness. Pp. 309-331 in D.I. Mostofsky (Ed.), *Attention, Contemporary Theory and Analysis.* New York: Appleton-Century-Crofts.

Hoke, M., C. Pantev, K. Lehnertz, and B. Lutenhoner
1988   Pp. 142-145 in K. Atsumi, M. Kotani, S. Ueno, T. Katila (Eds.), *Biomagnetism '87, Proceedings of the 6th International Conference on Biomagnetism.* Tokyo: Denki University Press.

Holtzman, J.D.
1984   Interactions between cortical and subcortical visual areas: Evidence from human commissurotomy patients. *Vision Research* 24:801-813.

Iverson, L.L.
1979   The chemistry of the brain. *Scientific American* 241:134-149.

Jackson, H.
1864   Loss of speech. *London Hospital Reports* 388-471.

Johnson, R., Jr.
1987   The amplitude of the P300 component of the event-related potential: Review and synthesis. In P.K. Ackles, J.R. Jennings, and M.G.H. Coles (Eds.), *Advances in Psychophysiology*, Vol III. Greenwich, Conn.: JAI Press.

Johnson, R., Jr., and P. Fedio
1986   Pre- and post-surgical event-related potentials in epilepsy patients. *Psychophysiology* 23:444-445.

Jolicoeur, P., and S.M. Kosslyn
1983   Coordinate systems of visual long-term memory representations. *Cognitive Psychology* 15:301-345.

Jouandet, M.L., M.S. Gazzaniga, J. Bazell, and W.C. Loftus
1987   Unfolding the human cerebral cortex into two dimensional maps. *Society for Neuroscience Abstracts* 13(Pt.2):352:2.

Jouandet, M.L., W.C. Loftus, J. Bazell, and M.S. Gazzaniga
in press   *Unfolding the Human Cerebral Cortex: Computer Generated Two-Dimensional Maps.* Cambridge: MIT Press.

Karis, D., D. Druckman, R. Lissak, and E. Donchin
1984   A psychophysiological analysis of bargaining: ERPs and facial expressions. In R. Karrer, J. Cohen, and P. Tueting (Eds.), *Brain and Information.* Annals of the New York Academy of Sciences, Volume 425.

Karis, D., M. Fabiani, and E. Donchin
1984   P300 and memory: Individual differences in the von Restorff effect. *Cognitive Psychology* 16:177-216.

Kornhuber, H.H., and L. Deecke
1965   Hirnpotential anerungen bei wilkurbewegungen und passiven bewegungen des menschen: Bereitschaftspotential und reafferente potentiale. *Pflugers Archi Fur Die Gestame Physiologie Des Menschen und Des Tierre* 284:1-17.

Kosslyn, S.M.
1980   *Image and Mind.* Cambridge, Mass.: Harvard University Press.
1987   Seeing and imagining in the cerebral hemispheres: A computational approach. *Psychological Review* 94:148-175.
1988   Aspects of a cognitive neuroscience of mental imagery. *Science* 240:1621-1626.

Kosslyn, S.M., J.D. Holtzman, M. Farah, and M.S. Gazzaniga
1985   A computational analysis of mental image generation: Evidence

from functional dissociations in split-brain patients. *Journal of Experimental Psychology: General* 114:311-341.

Kramer, A. (Ed.)
   1987   Psychophysiology and human factors. *Human Factors* Special Issue.

Kutas, M., and Hillyard, S.A.
   1980   Reading senseless sentences: Brain potentials reflect semantic incongruity. *Science* 207:203-205.
   1984   Brain potentials during reading reflect word expectancy and semantic association. *Nature* (London edition) 307:161-163.

Kutas, M., and C. Van Petten
   1987   Event-related brain potentials to grammatical errors and semantic anomalies. *Memory and Cognition* 11:539-550.

Kutas, M., G. McCarthy, and E. Donchin
   1977   Augmenting mental chronometry: The P300 as a measure of stimulus evaluation time. *Science* 197:792-795.

Lerner, R.M.
   1984   *On the Nature of Human Plasticity*. Cambridge: Cambridge University Press.

Lynch, A.B., and C.D. Baudry
   1988   Structure, function, relationships, and the organization of memory. In M.S. Gazzaniga (Ed.), *Perspectives in Memory Research*. Cambridge: MIT Press.

Marr, D.
   1982   *Vision*. San Francisco: W.H. Freeman.

Martin, W.R.W, W.J. Powers, and M.E. Raichle
   1987   Cerebral blood volume measured with inhaled $C^{15}O$ and positron emission tomography. *Journal of Cerebral Blood Flow and Metabolism* 7:421-426.

McCarthy, G., and E. Donchin
   1983   Chronometric analyses of human information processing. Pp. 251-268 in A.W.K., Gaillard and W. Ritter (Eds.), *Tutorials in Event-Related Potential Research: Endogenous Components. Advances in Psychology*, Vol. 10, G.E. Stelmach and P.A. Voon (Eds.). Amsterdam: North Holland Publishing Co.

McGeer, P.L.
   1983   The role of imaging in health care—A look at the future. Pp. 181-195 in *National Conference on Biological Imaging II. Clinical Aspects*. Papers presented at the conference. Washington, D.C.: National Academy Press.

Milner, B.
   1970   Memory and the medial temporal regions of the brain. In K.H. Pribram and D.E. Broadbent (Eds.), *Biology of Memory*. New York: Academic Press.

Mintun, M.A., M.E. Raichle, W.R.W. Martin, and P. Herscovitch
   1984   Brain oxygen utilization measured with O-15 radiotracers and positron emission tomography. *Journal of Nuclear Medicine* 25:177-187.

Mishkin, M.
   1982   A memory system in the monkey. *Philos. Trans. R. Soc. Lond. B Biol. Sci* 298:85-95.

REFERENCES

Naatanen, R.
1982 Processing negativity: An evoked potential reflection of selective attention. *Psychological Bulletin* 92:605-640.

Naatanen, R. and T. Picton
1987 The N1 wave of the human electric and magnetic response to sound: A review and an analysis of the component structure. *Psychophysiology* 24:375-425.

Nass, R.D., and M.S. Gazzaniga
1987 Cerebral lateralization and specialization in human central nervous system. In F. Plum (Ed.), *Handbook of Physiology*. Baltimore: Williams and Wilkins.

Neisser, U.
1967 *Cognitive Psychology*. New York: Appleton-Century Crofts.

Neville, H.J., M. Kutas, G. Chesney, and A.L. Schmidt
1986 Event-related brain potentials during initial encoding and recognition memory of congruous and incongruous words. *Journal of Memory and Language* 25:75-92.

Newell, A., and H.S. Simon
1972 *Human Problem Solving*. Englewood Cliffs, N.J.: Prentice-Hall.

Nunez, P.
1981 Electric fields of the brain: The neurophysics of EEG. New York: Oxford University Press.

Okada, Y.C., and C. Nicholson
1988 Magnetic evoked fields associated with transcortical currents in turtle cerebellum. *Biophysiology Journal* 53:723-31.

Okada, Y.C., M. Lauritzen, and C. Nicholson
1987 Magnetic fields associated with neural activity in an isolated cerebellum. *Brain Research* 412:151-155.

Okada, Y.C., L. Kaufman, and S.J. Williamson
1982 Hippocampal formation as a source of endogenous slow potentials. *EEG and Clin. Neurophysiol.* 55:417-426.

Pelizzone, M., S.J. Williamson, and L. Kaufman
1985 Evidence for multiple areas in the human auditory cortex. Pp. 326-330 in H. Weinberg, G. Stroink, and T. Katila (Eds.), *Biomagnetism: Applications and Theory*. New York: Pergamon.

Penfield, W., and L. Roberts
1959 *Speech and Brain Mechanisms*. Princeton, N.J.: Princeton University Press.

Perlmutter, J.S., K.B. Larson, M.E. Raichle, J. Markham, M.A. Mintun, M.R. Kilbourn, and M.J. Welch
1986 Strategies for in vivo measurement of receptor binding using positron emission tomography. *Journal of Cerebral Blood Flow and Metabolism* 6:154-169.

Petersen, S.E., P.T. Fox, M. Posner, M.A. Mintun, and M.E. Raichle
1988 Positron emission tomographic studies of the cortical anatomy of single word processing. *Nature* (in press).

Phelps, M.E., S.C. Huang, E.J. Hoffman, C. Selin, L. Sokoloff, and D.E. Kuhl
1979 Tomographic measurement of local cerebral glucose metabolic rate in humans with ^{18}F-2-fluoro-2-deoxyglucose: Validation of method. *Annals of Neurology* 6:371-388.

Posner, M.I., S.E. Petersen, P.T. Fox, and M.E. Raichle
  1988   Localization of cognitive functions in the human brain. *Science* (in press).
Prichard, J.W., and R.G. Shulman
  1986   NMR spectroscopy of brain metabolism in vivo. *Annals of Review of Neuroscience* 9:61-85.
Pritchard, W.S.
  1981   Psychophysiology of P300. *Psychological Bulletin* 89:506-540.
Pylyshyn, Z.W.
  1979   Validating computational models: A critique of Anderson's indeterminancy of representation claim. *Psychological Review* 86:383-394.
Raichle, M.E.
  1983   Positron emission tomography. *Annals of Review of Neuroscience* 6:249-268.
  1987   Circulatory and metabolic correlates of brain function in normal humans. *Handbook of Physiology, the Nervous System v. Higher Functions of the Brain.* Bethesda, Md.: American Physiological Society.
Raichle, M.E., W.R.W. Martin, P. Herscovitch, M. Mintun, and J. Markham
  1983   Brain blood flow measured with $H_2 15_O$. II. Implementation and validation. *Journal of Nuclear Medicine* 24:790-798.
Reivich, M., D. Kuhl, A. Wolf, J. Greenberg, M. Phelps, T. Ido, N. Cosella, J. Fowler, E. Hoffman, A. Alavi, P. Som, and L. Sokoloff
  1979   The ^{18}fluorodeoxyglucose method for the measurement of local cerebral glucose metabolism in man. *Circulation Research* 44:127-137.
Ricci, G.B., R. Leoni, G.L. Romani, F. Campitelli, S. Bunomo, and I. Modena
  1985   3-D neuromagnetic localization of sources of interictal activity in cases of focal epilepsy. Pp. 304-310 in H. Weinberg, G. Stroink, and T. Katila (Eds.), *Biomagnetism: Applications and Theory.* New York: Pergamon Press.
Romani, G.L., S.J. Williamson, and L. Kaufman
  1982   Tonotopic organization of the human auditory cortex. *Science* 216:1339-1340.
Rossler, S.
  1983   Endogenous ERPs and cognition: Probes, prospects, pitfall in matching pieces for the mind-body puzzle. *Tutorials in ERP Research: Endogenous Components.* Amsterdam: North Holland Publishing.
Rumelhart, D.E., and J.L. McClelland (Eds.)
  1986   *Parallel Distributed Processing*, Vols. I and II. Cambridge, Mass.: MIT Press.
Scherg, M., and D. Von Carmon
  1985   A new interpretation of the generators of baep waves I-IV: Results of a spatio-temporal dipole model. *Journal of Electroencephalography and Clinical Neurophysiology* 62:290-299.
Shepard, R.N., and L.A. Cooper
  1982   *Mental Images and Their Transformations.* Cambridge, Mass.: MIT Press.

REFERENCES

Simon, D.P., and H.A. Simon
    1978   Individual differences in problem solving. Pp. 325-348 in R.S. Siegler (Ed.), *Children's Thinking: What Develops?* Hillsdale, N.J.: Erlbaum.

Skrandies, W., and D. Lehmann
    1982   Spatial principal components of multichannel maps evoked by lateral visual half-field stimuli. *Electroencephalography and Clinical Neurophysiology* 54:297-305.

Sokoloff, L., M. Rivich, C. Kennedy, M.H. De Rosiers, C.S. Patlak, K.C. Pettigrew, O. Sakurada, and M. Shinohara
    1977   The ^{14}C-deoxyglucose method for the measurement of local cerebral glucose utilization: Theory, procedure, and normal values in the conscious and anesthetized albino rat. *Journal of Neurochemistry* 28:897-916.

Squire, L.R.
    1987   Memory: Neural organization and behavior. In *Handbook of Physiology*. Bethesda, Md.: American Physiological Society.

Sternberg, S.
    1969   Memory-scanning: Mental processes revealed by reaction-time experiments. *American Scientist* 4:421-457.

Swinney, K.R., and J.P. Wikswo, Jr.
    1980   A calculation of the magnetic field of a nerve action potential. *Biophys. J.* 32:719-731.

Swinney, D., E. Zuriff, and J. Nicol
    1989   The effects of focal brain damage on sentence processing: Examinations of neurological organization of a mental module. *Journal of Cognitive Neuroscience* 1(1):25.

Treisman, A.
    1969   Strategies and models of selective attention. *Psychol. Rev.* 76: 282-299.

Ullman, S.
    1984   Visual routines. *Cognition* 18:97-159.

Van Essen, D.C. and J.H.R. Maunsell
    1980   Two dimensional maps of the cerebral cortex. *The Journal of Comparative Neurology* 191:255-281.

Van Petten, C., and M. Kutas
    1987   Ambiguous words in context: An event-related analysis of the time course of meaning activation. *Journal of Memory and Language* 26:188-208.

Wagner, H.N., D. Burns, R.F. Dannals
    1983   Imaging dopamine receptors in the human brain by positron tomography. *Science* 221:1264-1266.

Walter, W.G., R. Cooper, A.J. Aldridge, W.C. McCallum, and A.L. Winter
    1964   Contingent negative variation: An electrical sign of sensorimotor association and expectancy in the human brain. *Nature* 203:380-384.

Weiskrantz, L., E.R. Warrington, M.D. Sanders, and J. Marshall
    1974   Visual capacity in the hemianopic field following a restricted occipital ablation. *Brain* 97:709-728.

Wernicke, C.
    1864   Der aphasische symptomencomplex, eine psychologische studie auf anatomischer basis. Breslau: Cohn and Weigert.

Williamson, S.J., and L. Kaufman
    in press Analysis of electromagnetic signals. In A. Redmond and A. Gevins (Eds.), *Handbook of Electroencephalography and Clinical Neurophysiology*. Amsterdam: Elsevier.

Winston, P.H. (Ed.)
    1978   *The Psychology of Computer Vision.* New York: McGraw Hill.

Wurtz, R.H., and J.E. Albano
    1980   Visual-motor function of the primate superio colliculus. *Annals of Rev. Neurosci* 3:189-226.

Wurtz, R.H., M.E. Goldberg, and D.L. Robinson
    1980   *Prog. Psychobiol. Physiol. Psychol.* 9:43-83.

Zuriff, E.B., and A. Caramazza
    1976   Psycholinguistic structure in aphasia: Studies in syntax and semantics. In H. Whitaker and H. Whitaker (Eds.), *Studies in Neurolinguistics*. New York: Academic Press.